Parallels and Paradoxes

EXPLORATIONS IN MUSIC AND SOCIETY

Daniel Barenboim and Edward W. Said

Edited and with a Preface by Ara Guzelimian

BLOOMSBURY

First published in Great Britain 2003
This paperback edition published 2004

Copyright © 2002 by Edward W. Said
Preface and Afterword copyright © Ara Guzelimian

The moral right of the author has been asserted

The pieces below were originally published in the following:

"Barenboim and the Wagner Taboo" (*Al Hayat*, August 15, 2001)
"Daniel Barenboim and Edward W. Said: A Dialogue"
(*Grand Street*, Issue 70, 2002)
"Daniel Barenboim and Edward W. Said: A Conversation"
(*Raritan*, Summer 1998)

Grateful acknowledgement is made to *The New York Review of Books*
for permission to reprint "German, Jews and Music" by Daniel
Barenboim (*The New York Review of Books*, March 29, 2001).
Copyright © 2001 by NYREV, Inc. Reprinted by permission of The
New York Review of Books

Bloomsbury Publishing Plc, 38 Soho Square, London W1D 3HB

A CIP catalogue record for this book is available from
the British Library

ISBN 0 7475 6385 3

10 9 8 7 6 5

All papers used by Bloomsbury Publishing are natural, recyclable
products made from wood grown in well-managed forests.
The manufacturing processes conform to the
environmental regulations of the country of origin.

Printed in Great Britain by Clays Ltd, St Ives plc

To the young musicians of the West-Eastern Divan Workshop

Contents

Contents

Preface
by Ara Guzelimian

"You *must* meet my friend Edward Said!"

Daniel Barenboim was most emphatic about that. He and I had just had the first substantial conversation of our acquaintance, working on various aspects of a Carnegie Hall *Perspectives* project that explored his multifaceted musical interests and collaborations. With his boundless curiosity about everything around him, he began to pepper me with questions on my personal history. The moment he discovered my own Middle Eastern origins, he insisted on introducing me immediately to Edward Said.

The friendship between Edward Said and Daniel Barenboim dates back a decade earlier to a chance meeting in a London hotel lobby in the early 1990s and has blossomed into an extraordinary collaboration. A passion for music and ideas is surely the binding force, but there is also the powerful underlying pull of parallel personal geographies. Both men come from a complex overlapping of cultures.

Edward Said was born in Jerusalem into a Palestinian family, but grew up largely in Cairo, once removed already from his origins. As a member of a rather anglicized Christian Arab family living in a predominantly Muslim society, he was arguably displaced once more. And he was displaced yet again to the United States where, as a teenager, he attended boarding school. Even his father's history is geographically complex. Prior to Edward's birth, Wadie Said had lived for a time in the United States, had attained American citizenship, and had even fought in the United States Army before returning to Palestine and Egypt. That peripatetic nature is readily found in many Middle Eastern family histories.

Daniel Barenboim's background is just as complex. He was born into a Russian Jewish family that immigrated during his grandparents' generation to Buenos Aires, where there was a thriving Jewish population, the third largest of any city in the world at the time. He subsequently immigrated with his parents to the newly created state of Israel, and his homes since that time have included London, Paris, Jerusalem, Chicago, and Berlin.

In each case, music was a formative and defining passion, fueled by recordings and the surprisingly rich musical life to be found in Cairo and Buenos Aires in the years following World War II. When Daniel Barenboim drew me into their friendship, it was partly in immediate recognition of striking parallels in my own background. I was born into an Armenian family in Cairo and many of my earliest memories are musical ones—my brother playing Bach Inventions for his piano lessons or the entire family going to a concert at the original Cairo Opera House (for which Verdi wrote *Aida*), where I remember seeing an ornate white piano reputed to have belonged to King Farouk. My parents attended some of the same memorable concerts and operas as the teenage Edward Said and, in fact, my mother remembers well the stationery store owned by Edward's father.

Preface

Edward Said is now best known as an extraordinarily influential and innovative intellectual force, an astute commentator on literature and culture, on culture's relationship to society, particularly in examining questions of Orientalism, a field of studies which he has pioneered. He is also a most forceful and impassioned commentator on the endlessly complex conflicts in the Middle East. But music still remains essential in his intellectual and personal life. He has written an enormous body of musical essays, and he remains an accomplished pianist.

As music director of both the Chicago Symphony Orchestra and the Deutsche Staatsoper in Berlin, Daniel Barenboim is a central figure in the musical world. He is one of the most recorded artists in history, with a nearly fifty-year span of recordings dating back to his earliest discs made when he was in his teens. He has taken numerous highly public and courageous stands, becoming an outspoken advocate for the performance of Wagner's music in Israel, fighting the lingering presence of anti-Semitism in Germany's cultural politics, and becoming the first and most prominent Israeli musician ever to perform in the Palestinian West Bank (an invitation organized, not surprisingly, by Edward Said).

The Barenboim/Said friendship has had numerous fruitful public manifestations. In 1999, the two were central to a bold experiment in bringing together Israeli and Arab musicians to Weimar, Germany, as part of a celebration of the 250th anniversary of Goethe's birth. That Weimar workshop has since been repeated both in Germany and in Chicago. Edward Said adapted and wrote a connective narrative for Daniel Barenboim's concert performances in Chicago of Beethoven's *Fidelio,* as well as the program essay for the subsequent Barenboim/Berlin recording of the opera. They have held numerous public dialogues on various musical topics, two of which were the starting point of this current book.

The conversations in this book took place over the span of five years. They are a selective and necessarily compressed distillation of an ongoing dialogue between two extraordinary creative minds.

My thanks go, first of all, to Edward Said and Daniel Barenboim for the enormous pleasure of their company, both in person and on paper. All three of us also owe a debt of gratitude to our editor, Shelley Wanger, for her encouragement, tempered with a discerning critical eye. Our thanks also to Patrick Sharpe for his meticulous transcription of hours of conversation, as well as to Professor David Freedberg and Francesca Nespoli of Columbia University's Casa Italiana for providing a conducive setting for several of these conversations. Zaineb Istrabadi, Sandra Fahy, John Deverman, and Antje Werkmeister helped in countless ways, especially by keeping all of us in regular contact during the almost constant travels of Messrs. Said and Barenboim. Henry Fogel, Osvaldo Golijov, Alexa Nieschlag, and Matias Tarnopolsky all contributed helpful suggestions and corrections in various stages of the book. And finally, my enduring thanks to my wife, Jan, and to our son, Alec, for their love and their willingness to turn over our dining table to innumerable piles of annotated manuscript pages.

New York
February 6, 2002

Introduction

Two of the conversations in this book took place in front of audiences in New York and therefore have the character of trying to keep a large audience interested. The earliest was held at Columbia University's Miller Theater in October 1995, as an event in an academic weekend conference about Richard Wagner. The idea was to take advantage of Daniel Barenboim's brief presence in the city and to use it to draw him out in public about his many years of conducting Wagner in Bayreuth, Berlin, Chicago, Salzburg, and several other places. What added value to the conversation was that Daniel was the only musician participating in the conference, and therefore brought an essential and certainly a practical perspective to what would otherwise have been a purely academic occasion.

The other public dialogue we had five years later was arranged for and moderated by our mutual friend Ara Guzelimian, Artistic Advisor of Carnegie Hall, who brought us together on the stage of Carnegie's Weill Recital Hall during a break in a series of concerts by the Chicago Symphony Orchestra conducted by Daniel.

Partly because we had both enjoyed and benefited from

Introduction

our initial Wagner dialogue in 1995, we continued to meet in the intervening years and record a series of more conversations about music, culture, and politics during those rare periods when we were together for long enough in the same place. (All of these conversations took place before September 11.) At first we started our conversations by ourselves, with only a tape-recorder turning silently in the background. Although they were intermittent and took place both in New York and during August 1999 in Weimar, we found that a number of themes kept recurring that reflected our own professional interests, Daniel as a performing pianist and conductor, myself as a teacher and writer for whom music has been an important part of my life. We therefore had many more tapes than we ultimately used for this book, for the simple reason that repetition, hesitation, the sometimes slow process of exploring a new subject tentatively and painstakingly, as well as just long-windedness necessarily appeared in what we said to each other in the privacy of our company. There was no audience to capture or amuse. After all, we reasoned, as close friends with all sorts of overlapping concerns (not the least of them being the fact that each of us—Daniel the Israeli, myself the Palestinian—had his eye on the unfolding Oslo peace process, with different expectations and, in the beginning at least, with different perspectives), we were together exploring the parallels as well as the paradoxes of our lives saying, in effect, what's wrong with doing it in our own unself-conscious way? Later, as the idea of publishing our conversations drew the attention of friends and editors, we thought it would be wonderful if we could persuade a mutual friend who knew a great deal about music and our part of the world to join us, so that we could give shape and discipline to the unfolding discussions.

Everything changed for the better when Ara Guzelimian

joined us in December 2000. I was in the throes of treatment while also trying to continue with my teaching at Columbia, Daniel was performing all the Beethoven symphonies and concerti for piano (he was the soloist) with his German orchestra, the Berlin Staatskapelle, in Carnegie Hall. We found time on successive days to schedule several hours of discussion (sensitively and intuitively guided by Ara), much of it about Beethoven. I felt that it was a rare and wonderful thing to elicit reflections about music from a great musician at the very height of his powers during a week when he was traversing a major oeuvre (some would say *the* major oeuvre) of Western music. Being an informal and unpompous individual, Daniel responded generously to the needs of the discussion, which was fed all the time, I think, by the steady flow of Beethoven's music, in all its drama, complexity, and intensity, that kept sounding in our collective ears in the background.

What the reader now holds in her/his hands has been culled from these lengthy and charged exchanges by Ara Guzelimian. It is therefore imperative that our remarks be read and understood not as ex cathedra musicological and aesthetic statements about music generally, Beethoven's in particular, but rather as a record of the kind of concerns and subjects stimulated by hearing (Ara and myself) and performing (Daniel) most of Beethoven's great orchestral and concerted works each evening for a week and a half.

About eight years ago I clearly remember asking Daniel, who had just finished conducting a blazing performance of Wagner's *Tristan und Isolde,* whether the music continued sounding in his ears (as it did in mine) while we sat chatting over dinner after the performance. "In fact," I added, "I can't stop hearing that searingly romantic and audacious sound constantly: it's almost driving me crazy." "No," he responded definitively, "I just cut it off, and now I am talking and having dinner with you." And indeed that's exactly what he seemed to be doing, even though for me the mystery of performance, memory, and extraordinary sustained sound gripped my attention for quite a long time. I wasn't at all persuaded that for him *Tristan* had just ended, although of course we did have a coherent and rational conversation on subjects about as far from *Tristan*'s almost suffocatingly cloistral world as one could be. What I found myself doing in our sometimes bantering, sometimes very serious conversation, however, were two things: one, I was trying to understand what and how *he* had done what he had with *Tristan,* which I had just witnessed and could remember, even if I was trying to do so indirectly through conversation; and two, I was also trying to find analogies in my work that would help me better grasp his. I should say also that having been a serious amateur musician and pianist all of my life, this kind of protracted encounter, which turned into a great friendship for both of us, became a very rich thing.

I hope that the written and distilled record of some of our conversations here will prove enjoyable to the reader. In no way is what follows intended as an academic or professional contribution to discussions about the nature of art and life, or to the immense amount of gossip that already exists about the world of performers and the music business. Our hope is to provide our readers with an account of spontaneous face-to-face interactions between two active individuals who are close friends and have full and busy lives that intersect in all sorts of unexpected and, we think, illuminating ways. Our whole aim was to share our thoughts amiably and energetically with each other, and with others for whom music, culture, and politics today form a unique whole. What that whole is, I am happy to say, neither of us can fully state, but we ask our readers, our friends, to join us in trying to find out. After all, these are conversations not treatises, and it is the nature of conversation at its best to be engrossing for everyone involved, as well as from time to time to take even the speaker by surprise.

E.W.S.
New York
March 2002

Parallels and Paradoxes

Chapter One

———∞∞∞———

Ara Guzelimian: I want to begin by asking each of you: Where are you at home? Or do you ever feel at home? Do you feel yourself in perpetual motion?

Daniel Barenboim: The used and abused cliché "I am at home wherever I make music" is true. I say "used and abused" because many of my colleagues and I have used this cliché on occasions when we didn't know exactly how to answer this very question or didn't want to be rude in places that were very hospitable to us yet didn't make us feel at home. Wherever I can play the piano—preferably with a reasonably good instrument—or wherever I travel with the orchestras that I lead, the Chicago Symphony Orchestra or the Staatskapelle from Berlin, I feel at home.

I feel at home in a certain way in Jerusalem, but I think this is a little bit unreal, a poetic idea with which I grew up. We moved to Israel when I was ten years old and lived in Tel Aviv, which is a city without any history to speak of, a very modern city, not particularly interesting, but bustling and bubbling with life. Whereas Jerusalem, of course, means everything to so many different people, and this is why its politics have always been so problematic. And in the 1950s, Tel Avivians looked to Jerusalem for everything that they couldn't find in their own city: spirituality, intellectual and cultural curiosity. All those things now unfortunately seem to be disappearing due to the lack of tolerance shown by some of the extreme populations in Jerusalem.

So what I mean to say is that I feel at home in the *idea* of Jerusalem. Otherwise, I feel at home in the company of a very few close friends. And, I must say, Edward to me has become the one friend with whom I can share so many things, a soul mate. I feel very at home whenever I am with him.

I am not a person who cares very much for possessions. I don't care much about furniture, or reminiscences from the past. I don't collect memorabilia—so my feeling of being at home somewhere is really a feeling of transition, as everything is in life. Music is transition, too. I am happiest when I can be at peace with the idea of fluidity. And I'm unhappy when I cannot really let myself go and give myself over completely to the idea that things change, evolve, and not necessarily for the best.

Edward W. Said: One of my earliest memories is of homesickness, of wishing that I was somewhere else. But over time, I've come to view the idea of home as being overrated. There's a lot of sentimentality about "homelands" that I don't really care for. And wandering around is really what I like to do most. But the reason I find myself so happy in New York is that New York is a chameleon city. You can be anywhere *in* it and still not be *of* it. In some ways I appreciate that.

When I travel, particularly when I return to where I grew up in the Middle East, I find myself thinking about all the resistance I feel to going back. When I went back, for example, to Jerusalem in 1992 with my family I found it a completely different place. I hadn't been there for nearly forty-five years, and it's just not the same place I recall, and of course the Palestine where I spent part of my youth became Israel. I didn't grow up in the West Bank, and so a place like Ramallah, a wonderful location where Daniel played his recital at the Palestinian conservatory a year or so ago, is really not home to me. I feel very much at home in a place like Cairo, where I spent most of my formative years. Cairo has something of the eternal about it. It's a fantastically complicated and sophisticated city, and its particular dialect is what profoundly appeals to me in the end.

I think one of the things that Daniel and I have in common is a fixation on the ear rather than on the eye. Like Daniel, I'm not attached to physical objects as such, except I collect certain things. I have a good-sized collection of fountain pens for reasons that have to do with my father's profession. As a follower of Kant, I hate computers. I collect pipes and clothes, but that's about it. Possessions don't inspire the same feelings in me that they would in a collector of art or houses or cars. I've read about people who have fifty cars. That's incomprehensible to me.

Daniel mentioned—and I ended my memoir *Out of Place* with a similar thought, which I think is quite important—the sense that identity is a set of currents, flowing currents, rather than a fixed place or a stable set of objects. I certainly feel that about myself.

DB: This idea of "currents" must be related to the way you've lived your life. You were born in Jerusalem, which was British at the time; you grew up in Cairo, which was British at the time. Then it became Egyptian, and you immigrated to America. A very high percentage of your interests are European. The things that matter to you the most—what you think, what you teach, what you know, not only in literature, in philosophy, in history, but in music—most of these are European in origin.

If one is active in a profession which is more than a profession, which is a way of life, as it is for us—beyond nine to five—then geographical location is less important. I'm sure that when you read Goethe, you feel, in a funny way, German, as I do when conducting Beethoven or Bruckner. This was one of the lessons of our workshop in Weimar. Precisely that it's not only possible to have multiple identities, but also, I would say, something to aspire toward. The sense of belonging to different cultures can only be enriching.

AG: Let's talk about the Weimar workshop. In 1999, the two of you collaborated in Weimar, Germany, which had been named the Culture Capital of Europe, a rotating honor given to different cities. On the 250th anniversary of Goethe's birth and in a city closely associated with Goethe, you brought together Arab and Israeli musicians, and a smaller group of German musicians as well, to play as one orchestra. I'd like to ask both of you what you hoped to achieve in doing this and, in the end, what you felt was achieved.

EWS: In a way it was a quite daring experiment. There have been attempts in the past—I know in this country they've brought musicians from Arab countries and Israel to play together in music camps and give concerts—but the novelty of Weimar was, first of all, the level of participation at the top: it included Daniel and Yo-Yo Ma. You can't find any better musicians to lead a group like this. Most of the participants were between the ages of eighteen and twenty-five, although I do remember that there was a cellist who was fourteen or fifteen, a Kurdish boy from Syria.

It took quite a long time to prepare for the event. Of course it required auditions. And it was not surprising that, at least in some Arab countries, there was a question of whether the governments would allow the students to attend. They all did come in the end, including a group from Syria, a group from Jordan, one from the Palestinian territories, and others from Israel, Egypt, Lebanon, and maybe one or two other countries.

There was an assumption that this program might be an alternative way of making peace. The peace process, as I have said at great and turgid length elsewhere, doesn't seem to be bringing results. But I don't think saving the peace process was our main intention. From my point of view, the idea was to see what would happen if you brought these people together to play in an orchestra in Weimar, in the spirit of Goethe, who wrote a fantastic collection of poems based on his enthusiasm for Islam. Goethe discovered Islam through Arabic and Persian sources—a German soldier who had been fighting in one of the Spanish campaigns in the early part of the nineteenth century brought back a page of the Koran for him. Goethe was transfixed. He started to learn Arabic, although he didn't get very far. Then he discovered Persian poetry and produced this extraordinary set of poems about the "other" really, *West-östlicher Diwan (The West-Eastern Divan)*, which is, I think, unique in the history of European culture.

And that was the idea behind the experiment. And then, under that aegis, to bring the musicians together at Weimar, which is very close to Buchenwald, the terrible death camp. In fact, Buchenwald was *designed* to be near Weimar, which had been romanticized as the city at the very pinnacle of German culture: Goethe, Schiller, Wagner, Liszt, Bach all had lived there. Nobody could fully comprehend the proximity of such sublimity to such horror.

There was an orchestra rehearsal every day, in the morning and in the afternoon, led by Daniel of course. There were chamber music groups and master classes—all of them taking place simultaneously. Here were all these students, who had never seen each other before, and at night, several days a week, we would have discussions led by me about music, culture, politics, all sorts of things came up; no one felt under any pressure to hold back anything. And since the groups were so miscellaneous, both animosity and cordiality were almost always in evidence. The one thing that didn't happen was straight-out political fighting; there was an unwritten rule about that, at least so far as our evening discussions were concerned.

I remember the first discussion in particular because it immediately crystallized all the tensions that were in everybody's heart and mind. The conversation started by someone asking the group, "What do people feel about this whole thing?" One kid put up his hand and said, "I feel that I'm being discriminated against because I tried to join a group of improvisers and they wouldn't let me." So I asked, "What exactly happened?" A Lebanese violinist explained, "The problem is that after the program is over at night, usually around eleven o'clock, a group of us get together and improvise Arabic music." I turned to the first kid and asked him to explain the problem. He told me, "I'm an Albanian. I'm from Israel, but I'm originally from Albania and I'm Jewish, and they said to me 'You can't play Arabic music. Only Arabs can play Arabic music.'" It was quite an extraordinary moment. And there was this whole question about who could play Arabic music and who couldn't.

So that was one problem. And then, of course, the next question was, "Well, what gives you the right to play Beethoven? You're not German." So that discussion was going nowhere. There was an Israeli cellist in the audience who was also a soldier, and he was having trouble speaking in English, so Daniel asked him to speak in Hebrew. He more or less said, "I'm here to play music. I'm really not interested in all the other stuff that you guys are trying to push on us in these discussions about culture. I'm here to play music and I'm not interested in anything else and I feel very uncomfortable because, who knows, I might be sent to Lebanon and I'll have to fight some of these people." Daniel told him, "If you feel that uncomfortable, why don't you leave? Nobody's forcing you to stay." And he ended up staying.

So there was a very tentative atmosphere in the beginning. However, ten days later, the same kid who had claimed that only Arabs can play Arabic music was teaching Yo-Yo Ma how to tune his cello to the Arabic scale. So obviously he thought Chinese people could play Arabic music. Gradually the circle extended and they were all playing the Beethoven Seventh. It was quite an extraordinary event.

It was also amazing to watch Daniel drill this basically resistant group into shape. It wasn't only the Israelis and the Arabs who didn't care for each other. There were some Arabs who didn't care for other Arabs as well as Israelis who cordially disliked other Israelis. And it was remarkable to witness the group, despite the tensions of the first week or ten days, turn themselves into a real orchestra. In my opinion, what you saw had no political overtones at all. One set of identities was superseded by another set. There was an Israeli group, and a Russian group, and a Syrian group, a Lebanese group, a Palestinian group, and a group of Palestinian Israelis. All of them

9

suddenly became cellists and violinists playing the same piece in the same orchestra under the same conductor.

I will never forget the look of amazement on the part of the Israeli musicians during the first movement of Beethoven's Seventh where the oboist plays a very exposed A major scale. They all turned around to watch an Egyptian student play a perfect A major scale on the oboe—which Daniel had elicited out of him. The transformation of these kids from one thing to another was basically unstoppable.

DB: What seemed extraordinary to me was how much ignorance there was about the "other." The Israeli kids couldn't imagine that there are people in Damascus and Amman and Cairo who can actually play violin and viola. And I think the Arab musicians knew that there is a musical life in Israel, but they didn't know very much about it. One of the Syrian kids told me that he'd never met an Israeli before and, for him, an Israeli is somebody who represents a negative example of what can happen to his country and what can happen to the Arab world.

This same boy found himself sharing a music stand with an Israeli cellist. They were trying to play the same note, to play with the same dynamic, with the same stroke of the bow, with the same sound, with the same expression. They were trying to do something together. It's as simple as that. They were trying to do something together, something about which they both cared, about which they were both passionate. Well, having achieved that one note, they already can't look at each other the same way, because they have shared a common experience. And this is what was really, for me, the important thing about the encounter.

In the political world today, especially in Europe—I don't

want to say anything about American politics because I don't know enough about it—the leaders still behave as if they control the world, whereas in fact they hardly control anything. The world is controlled by big business and money. It seems to me that politicians are ultimately ineffectual and overcompensate with a public show of self-assurance. Obviously, money can buy a lot of things and, on occasion, at least for a short while, some goodwill. But the fact remains that if conflicts are one day to be solved, they are only going to be solved by contact between the warring parties.

The area that we're talking about—the Middle East—is very small. Contact is inevitable. It's not only dollars and political solutions about borders that are going to be the real test of whether a peaceful settlement will work or not. The real test is how productive this contact will be in the long run.

I believe that in cultural matters—with literature and, even better, with music, because it doesn't have to do with explicit ideas—if we foster this kind of a contact, it can only help people feel nearer to each other, and this is all.

EWS: One of the striking things about the kind of work you do is that you act as an interpreter, as a performer—an artist concerned not so much with the articulation of the self, but rather with the articulation of other selves. That's a challenge. The interesting thing about Goethe—and also about our experience in Weimar—was that art, for Goethe especially, was all about a voyage to the "other," and not concentrating on one self, which is very much a minority view today. There is more of a concentration today on the affirmation of identity, on the need for roots, on the values of one's culture and one's sense of belonging. It's become quite rare to project one's self outward, to have a broader perspective.

In your work as a performer, Daniel, and in my work as an interpreter—an interpreter of literature and literary criticism—one has to accept the idea that one is putting one's own identity to the side in order to explore the "other."

DB: I feel very much today—especially in the world of music, but not exclusively—that the choices are incorrect as presented. Let's go to the nerve of the question: the sound of the orchestra. Very often you hear, "Well, it's a pity that French orchestras have lost the nasal sound of the French bassoons. This is because they now play German bassoons. And the American orchestras sometimes play with German trumpets or trombones. And the Czech Philharmonic sounds very similar to the Sydney Symphony in sound, etc. What a terrible thing globalization is," people say. As if you have to be *French* to produce a nasal sound or *German* to produce the German sound.

This is absolutely the beginning of a lack of cultural tolerance. Yes, there is a difference between a feeling for national heritage and fascistic ideas about a nation-state. There was nothing wrong with the Germans in 1920 feeling that there was something very culturally *German* about Beethoven and Brahms. I have absolutely no problem with that. I begin to have a problem when they claim that only Aryans can appreciate Beethoven. And I think that this is where we're heading again.

The United States has proven the opposite, because the best American musicians don't relate to music on the level of culture. In other words, the great German musician will always have a visceral reaction to the Beethoven and Brahms that he or she grew up with, almost something atavistic from the stomach—which he or she will not have with *La Mer* by Debussy, even if the musician plays it marvelously. Whereas for the American musician, Beethoven and *La Mer* are equally distant or near, according to his talent and knowledge. Therefore, it is possible that each of us has the capacity to be many things.

EWS: One thing that is going around in this country, unfortunately, is a sort of amnesia about the fact that the United States is really an immigrant society, and always has been. And the attempts made recently to declare that America is one thing and not another, and the quarrel over what is the American tradition, and what is the canon, and what are the unifying aspects of America is a conversation that makes me deeply uncomfortable, because it can turn into a kind of imported sense of nationalism (what is "German," what is "English"). It has very little to do with the quite volatile and turbulent and finally, to me, deeply attractive aspects of America, which are that it's a society continually in a state of flux, continually in a state of unsettlement, rather than something that is given and formed once and for all. And, it seems to me, therefore, that places like the university or the orchestra—those places in the arts and sciences where one's life is given over to an ideal—should be places of exploration rather than places of simple affirmation and consolidation, which is really not at all, in my opinion, in conformity with the history of this society and this country.

DB: This is very much in your area, Edward. How do you explain that, on the one hand, market globalization makes everything the same. You can eat—

EWS: McDonald's. You can eat a Big Mac on the Champs-Élysées and in Cairo.

DB: And you don't have to go to Japan to eat sushi. And yet political conflicts and national conflicts are deeper and pettier than ever before. Why is that?

EWS: Well, there are two reasons. The first is the reaction *against* global homogenization. One way to defend yourself against the sense of an all-encompassing global atmosphere—represented by America, to most people—is to return to comfortable symbols of the past. In the Islamic world, for example, more people are wearing traditional dress, not necessarily as a form of piety, but as a way of affirming an identity that resists this global wave.

Second is the legacy of empires. In the case of the British, whenever they were forced to leave a place, they divided it up. It happened in India. It happened in Palestine. It happened in Cyprus. It happened in Ireland. The idea of *partition* as a quick way of solving the problem of multiple nationalities. It's like someone telling you, "Okay, the way to learn a musical piece is to divide it into tinier and tinier units, and then suddenly you can put it all together." It doesn't work that way. When you divide something up, it's not so easy to put it all back together.

Both of these factors have produced xenophobia and identity conflict which are endemic to modernity and very dangerous.

AG: I want to turn the subject to a musical figure who is formative and central to both of you—Wilhelm Furtwängler. That may seem like a radical right turn from where we just were, but it's related to our discussion of cultural influences. Growing up in Buenos Aires, Daniel saw a veritable parade of the greatest imaginable European musicians. It was the same in Cairo during the 1940s, 1950s, and a year or two in the 1960s. A thriving colonial European culture in Egypt dates much further back, to the establishment of the Cairo Opera House and the premiere of Verdi's *Aida*. It was quite possible to see Beniamino Gigli, Gino Bechi, and Maria Caniglia perform in Cairo in the 1940s. There were regular visits of out-of-season Italian and French opera troupes—

EWS: Out of shape too!

AG: Yes, and out of shape. Wilhelm Furtwängler and the Berlin Philharmonic came to Cairo in 1951. My parents were at those concerts, as was a teenage Edward Said. The broadcasts of a couple of Furtwängler's performances on Radio Cairo have survived—the Tchaikovsky Sixth Symphony and Bruckner Seventh Symphony—and there's a wonderful photograph of Wilhelm Furtwängler sitting on a camel, wearing a fez in front of the pyramids, which speaks volumes.

There's another photograph, reproduced in Daniel's book, *A Life in Music,* which shows Daniel, his back to the camera, wearing white shorts, framed by his parents, talking to Wilhelm Furtwängler. This was in Salzburg in 1954, when he was eleven or twelve years old. Furtwängler was so taken by Daniel's talent that he wrote a now famous letter inviting him to perform with the Berlin Philharmonic. Daniel's family, for reasons that maybe he will explain, declined. And, sadly, several months later, Furtwängler was dead.

I'd love to ask each of you just to begin with a personal account of your relationship to Furtwängler.

EWS: You mention the cultural life of Cairo in the 1940s and 1950s—well, I grew up hearing stories of Cairo in the 1930s as well, when it was a great venue for concerts, and many wonderful musicians passed through. A teacher of mine in Cairo named Ignace Tiegerman used to tell the story that Arthur Rubinstein gave a concert and enjoyed it so much that he wanted to give another in order to stay in Cairo a little longer. But they couldn't fit him in the concert calendar. It was so crowded, there was simply no place for him to play. So that was the sense of bustle that one had in those days. And I recall that when Furtwängler appeared, I had never seen what was, in effect, a great foreign orchestra. There were local groups playing and I would occasionally go to them, but they couldn't compare.

DB: Did you ever hear the Palestine Philharmonic?

EWS: Never. My parents heard them, however, and often spoke of the experience especially when Toscanini conducted them in Cairo. But I was considered too young for a concert when Toscanini visited in the forties.

Furtwängler's appearance in Cairo had been preceded the year before by the Vienna Philharmonic with Clemens Krauss, who came and played in the same cinema. And that was, for me, a wonderful experience, because although I'd been to the opera in Cairo and had experienced these overweight and out-of-shape singers—who were, in their own day, very great singers—going through the Italian repertory, the appearance of Krauss was extremely exciting.

But that experience was completely overshadowed by the appearance of Furtwängler and the Berlin Philharmonic. I had never in my life seen such concentration as was present on that stage. Furtwängler played a very conventional program, which duplicated standard works on some of the recordings we had at home. To hear the recordings come to life, as it were, was, for me, a tremendous thing. And this rather gaunt and unprepossessing figure on the podium was something very different from Clemens Krauss, who was almost like a businessman who just happened to be conducting. Furtwängler transfixed me with his frenetically waving arms and his tall, angular frame. And the thing that I remember, in particular, was his feeling for time. It was a new concept of time, because, for me, time had always been connected to duty and chores and things I was supposed to do. Here, all of a sudden, time was transformed into all the possibilities of organized musical sound and a beautiful plasticity, which I'd never before experienced in quite that way and with such a large number of people all at once.

Later, of course, I discovered Furtwängler again through writing and recordings, but in the Egyptian culture of that time, there wasn't really a place where I could look for anything about him. It was as if he were an *emanation*. Furtwängler existed in the European context. Here was a great figure from another culture transplanted into Cairo—a culture in transition—making this tremendous impression on individuals, and perhaps collectively on an audience, but there was no resonance beyond that. I remember feeling deprived because his performance had been a one-time experience. Perhaps it's given me a taste for the actuality of performance. When you play, there's something rare about it because of its evanescence. It happens and it's over, and then you have to carry it around in your mind.

DB: I understand what you mean about performance from the other side: playing in surroundings where there's no follow-up. I remember playing once in Calcutta with the Calcutta Symphony Orchestra. First of all, it was terribly hot. Rehearsals started at seven o'clock in the morning, and I'm not a morning person. When I was told exactly when I had to wake up for rehearsal, I thought, "It must be because of the heat." But actually it wasn't the heat. It was simply that most of the musicians were amateurs and they worked in shops and other places and had to go to work at ten o'clock. In instances like this, one remembers the feeling of giving a performance.

As for not going to Berlin and giving a concert with Furtwängler—what he represented was fraught with many difficulties. My musical education had come mostly from my father, which I consider to be extremely beneficial in that I don't think I've really changed anything of what I learned from him. I didn't have the problem of different teachers. I didn't have to adapt to different methods. But I was not taught the kind of music-making that I heard with Furtwängler.

In the summer of 1952, when I was nine years old, I was invited to Salzburg by Igor Markevitch, who was giving the conductors' class. It was there that I played my first concert in Europe. At the end of the conductors' class, I played as a piano soloist with the orchestra. I remember quite well that I didn't admire Markevitch the same way I admired Furtwängler. He was much more interested in so-called clarity and in other repertory, in other ways of making music.

It was Edwin Fischer who said, "You must go and play for Furtwängler." So I was summoned to the old Festspielhaus to play an audition.

EWS: What did you play?

DB: I remember playing the Bach Italian Concerto. I remember playing the second movement of a Beethoven sonata. I remember playing Prokofiev's Second Sonata and a couple of Chopin Études. I was eleven years old.

EWS: No one's perfect.

DB: On the contrary, the imperfections have been growing ever since. Being fifty-seven years old myself now, I imagine that if an eleven-year-old child came and played all those things, I would be impressed. It would be ridiculous to pretend false modesty and say, "No, no." Somehow, I think Furtwängler really was quite taken. And then he asked me to improvise, which I did, and he tested my hearing. I mean, at the risk of sounding terribly cynical, I thought it was extraordinary from somebody who had great difficulties in hearing himself. He was unable to deal with this affliction. Hearing aids in those days were obviously not as developed as they are today, and he threw his away because it made him hear everything in one color.

Anyway, Furtwängler tested my ear by playing some chords, and with my back to the piano, I had to tell him the notes. And he was very impressed and asked me to play with the Berlin Philharmonic. I was eleven, and I hardly spoke any German, in any case, and his English was rather poor. My father told him that it was the greatest honor that he could have bestowed upon me, but we were a Jewish family living in Israel—this was just nine years after the end of the war and the Holocaust—and he didn't feel it was the right time. And he hoped that Furtwängler would understand.

Not only did Furtwängler understand but, without anybody asking, he wrote the famous letter, which opened innumerable doors in my professional life. It was Furtwängler who sent me to play for George Szell, who was conducting in Salzburg, and Karl Böhm. This has all become folkloric. I was then allowed to sit in at the rehearsals of *Don Giovanni*, the production conducted by Furtwängler that was the basis of the famous 1954 film.

I really got to know everything about Furtwängler and his philosophy of music through his writings and his recordings and, of course, through people that I've met who have known him and worked with him—old musicians from both the Vienna and Berlin Philharmonic Orchestras. And I came to realize that Furtwängler had been unfairly criticized in the United States for political reasons, and some other matters that were totally untrue.

As you may know, he was supposed to have been music director of the Chicago Symphony Orchestra in 1948, but a whole list of Jewish artists—practically a Who's Who of musicians in America—signed a letter saying that they would no longer play with the Chicago Symphony Orchestra if he were engaged there. I think they all signed it, with the exception of Yehudi Menuhin. Obviously Furtwängler didn't come.

Furtwängler was also criticized for his music. Every great artist has a personal way of making music, of course. But Furtwängler had his own *philosophy* of music based on paradoxes and extremes being a necessity in order to achieve an equilibrium—on extremes being essential to achieve a musical equivalent of the Greek "catharsis." Extremes as a necessity in starting the path from chaos to order. Extremes as an absolute necessity in achieving unity in music. All this was not only out of fashion, in the same way that it's out of fashion today—in that respect, nothing has changed—but also the idea behind his method was much too intellectual and much too complicated for many people to understand.

And the outward manifestations of Furtwängler's kind of music-making were, shall we say, more disturbing than the outward manifestations of more orderly musicians. In other words, it was obvious that, in Furtwängler's Beethoven and Brahms, there was a certain fluctuation in tempo. In Wagner it was tolerated, but in Beethoven and Brahms? If you don't understand the reason for this fluctuation and the reasons for the extremes, you notice only the outward manifestations—extreme dynamics, extreme tempos, and fluctuations of tempo. And that's very disturbing to some listeners.

He was criticized in the same way that Wagner had been criticized for his conducting and that Liszt had been criticized for his playing. You've seen this kind of criticism throughout the history of music. After Furtwängler came Sergiu Celibidache, another highly individualistic conductor. The same criticism was leveled at Claudio Arrau. And, I must say, in my small and modest way, I am very proud to belong to that small, elite group that has been criticized for these things.

Furtwängler understood the music philosophically. He understood that music is not about statements or about being. It's about becoming. It's not the statement of a phrase that is really important, but how you get there and how you leave it and how you make the transition to the next phrase.

EWS: Don't you think that what you're saying about Furtwängler relies on a deeper level of awareness and reception than what is being put forward in the music itself? There doesn't seem to be a prearranged method when you listen to Furtwängler. The impression his music gives me is that it's being worked out in the performance itself, and these extremes, as you call them, are really part of an ongoing process that takes you through the piece from the opening silence to the final silence at the end, in a way that you can't abstract from the performance and say, "This is the formula. It's clear. And it can be repeated in the same way."

You and I have disagreed about Glenn Gould in the past. In a certain way, Glenn Gould is predictable. You know how much I admire him. But there is a Glenn Gould *manner* which can be reproduced, not by others, but by him. The thing about Furtwängler that has always impressed me tremendously, and I even recall it dimly from fifty years ago, is a sense of a highly plastic process, or what you call *transition,* which seems to be working itself out right then and there. There's no prior statement. There's no program. It's all contained in the actual performance, which is, I think, very difficult for some audiences to accept.

DB: Furtwängler was not only spontaneous and flexible, you know.

EWS: No, it's not about spontaneity. I don't mean that.

DB: Furtwängler rehearsed sometimes very painstakingly and thoroughly, but he rehearsed in a different way. This is very well defined by Celibidache. He says that Furtwängler rehearsed two hundred ways of saying "no" in the hope that on the evening of the concert you can once say "yes." In other words, you rehearse to make sure that certain things don't happen. That the music doesn't sound hollow here, or drag there, that there's no accent in another place, whereas most people rehearse so that they can put it together in the morning and then repeat it in the evening. But the most extraordinary thing about music is its unrepeatability, if one can use that word.

EWS: That quality I mentioned earlier: something very rare.

DB: Sound is ephemeral. It goes by. One of the reasons why sound is so expressive is that it's not here at your beck and call. You can't draw the curtain and see it again like a painting or open it like a book. This quality is what Furtwängler understood and articulated. Some of his writings are very much tied to the Zeitgeist of his time, and some of his contentions about atonal music are very naïve. But his understanding of the nature of music is to my mind unique.

AG: Isn't this part of the perpetual Apollonian/Dionysian battle that has gone on for centuries in the arts? The quantifiable and ordered versus the irrational?

EWS: It's a common misunderstanding to pose this battle as an either/or—either you're Dionysian or you're Apollonian. Whereas Nietzsche argues that one requires the other. That's the difficult thing: the two are synthesized in special and privileged moments like tragedy, which, paradoxically, are painstakingly rehearsed and *not* something that happens in a kind of spontaneous or miraculous way. There is a certain science to it, you could say. It's generally true in the arts that what seems like a finished performance, whether it's a painting or a poem, really is anticipated by a great many processes, moments, choices that go on before the finished work is put before you. In literature, the words are shared by everyone. Everybody uses language. The words you see in a poem, play, or novel, although they're arranged in different ways and have a highly artistic finish to them, are the words of everyday life. I find music fascinating in part because it encompasses silence, even though it is, of course, made of sound. Music doesn't explain itself in the same way that a word does in relationship to other words.

This is one of the reasons why music today, at least in the West, is separate from the other arts. Music requires a particular type of education which is simply not given to most people. And, as a result, it's set further apart. It has a special place. People who are familiar with painting and photography and drama and dance, and so on, cannot talk so easily about music. And yet, as Nietzsche writes in *The Birth of Tragedy*, music is potentially the most accessible art form because, with the Apollonian and the Dionysian coming together, it makes a more powerful and involving impression than the other arts. And the paradox is that while music is accessible, it can't ever be understood.

DB: The other challenging notion about music is that it can serve two totally opposed purposes. If you want to forget everything and run away from your problems and difficulties—from sheer existence—music is the perfect means, because it's highly emotional. Music can lead to states of frenzy, as Wagner expected his *Tristan* to produce. Or lead to extreme feelings of savagery, as in Stravinsky's *The Rite of Spring*.

But, on the other hand, the study of music is one of the best ways to learn about human nature. This is why I am so sad about music education being practically nonexistent today in schools. Education means preparing children for adult life; teaching them how to behave and what kinds of human beings they want to be. Everything else is information and can be learned in a very simple way. To play music well you need to strike a balance between your head, your heart, and your stomach. And if one of the three is not there or is there in too strong a dose, you cannot use it. What better way than music to show a child how to be human?

If one observes the great works of music, or even lesser

works of music, one can learn to understand many things. The Fourth Symphony of Beethoven is not only a means of escaping from the world. There is a sense of total abyss when it starts, with one sustained note, a B-flat, one flute, the bassoons, the horns, and the *pizzicato,* the strings . . . and then nothing happens. There's this feeling of emptiness, only one note sticking there alone, and then the strings come in with another note, a G-flat, and at that moment, the listener is displaced.

I would argue that this sense of displacement is unique. When you hear the first note, you think, "Well, maybe this is going to be in B-flat." In the end it really *is* in B-flat, but by the second note you don't know where you are anymore because it's G-flat. From that moment alone you can understand so many things about human nature. You understand that things are not necessarily what they seem at first sight. B-flat is perhaps the key, but the G-flat introduces other possibilities. There's a static, immovable, claustrophobic feeling. Why? Because of the long, sustained notes. Followed by notes that are as long as the silences between them. The music reaches a low point from which Beethoven builds up the music all over again and finally affirms the key.

You might call this the road from chaos to order, or from desolation to happiness. I'm not going to linger on these poetic descriptions, because the music means different things to different people. But one thing is clear. If you have a sense of belonging, a feeling of home, harmonically speaking—and if you're able to establish that as a composer, and establish it as a musician—then you will always get this feeling of being in no-man's-land, of being displaced yet always finding a way home. Music provides the possibility, on the one hand, to escape from life and, on the other hand, to understand it much better than in many other disciplines. Music says, "Excuse me. This is human life."

AG: We have so far covered ideas and even formative influences where you have much in common with each other. Where do your views differ?

EWS: One area where Daniel and I disagree is that we have different views of the history of the part of the world from which we both come. That is to say, Daniel sees history from a point of view that is obviously different from that of a Palestinian. And in fact there is some value in keeping distinct different views of history without collapsing them into one another, and I think this tension can be healthy rather than unhealthy.

One of my criticisms of the peace process as it's currently being enacted on television screens and at negotiating tables is that, in a way, it's ahistorical. The process doesn't do enough to recognize the Palestinian narrative and what they went through, and it's sort of amnesiac about the need to understand history in its complexity and detail in order for people to be able to live with that history. And I think, for me, to pretend that history isn't important, and that we have to start somehow from the realities on the ground, is a pragmatic political notion that I simply can't agree with as a humanist and somebody who believes that peoples' histories are complex things involving ideas of justice and injury and oppression.

I don't think it's necessary that everyone should agree, as long as there's a mutual acknowledgment that a different view exists. That's the important thing. We must have respect for each other's views and tolerate each other's histories. Especially because, as Daniel said, we're talking about such a small part of the world. The idea of separating people simply cannot work—it hasn't worked. The moment you start boxing people in, you give them a sense of insecurity and produce more paranoia. You produce, in my opinion, more distortions.

It's the same anyplace. You know the story of the Lebanese civil war, which began as a conflict over large areas of territory and, in the end, was fought over individual streets and sidewalks. And where did it lead? Nowhere. So the idea of different but intertwined histories is crucial to a discussion—without necessarily resolving them into each other.

AG: I would imagine that this idea is a fundamental element of your friendship too, because you have inevitably intertwined histories and yet very different perspectives. From what I've observed, one of the pleasures of your dialogue is to wrestle with both the parallels and paradoxes.

New York,
March 8, 2000

Chapter Two

—⟨∞⟩—

EWS: There's no real equivalent of the performer in literature. Authors can read before a public, but the logical aim of what we do is to produce silence—silent readings. Now, in the case of a performing musician like you, the idea of performance is the end result of what you're doing.

DB: Yes, but the equivalent of somebody writing a book is not somebody performing a piece of music but rather writing one. In other words, I don't think you can compare a writer with a pianist. You have to compare a writer with a composer; although for the composer, in many ways, the ultimate goal is to get a performance of his works. But I think that there is a very clear difference between the whole process of preparing a work of music for performance and the performance itself. In a performance, you don't stop unless there is some unforeseen dramatic interruption. Once the piece starts, it goes to the end. And, therefore, it has to have a certain inevitability and a certain logical construction as far as volume, sound, and speed are concerned, which are not the same as in rehearsal, when you can stop and try to better things. A performance has only one possibility—in other words, the nature of sound being ephemeral, once it is over, it is finished. In the process of preparation, one has to take into account all these elements— the fact that it has to go to one goal. In other words, it is the sort of equivalent to the life of a human being or of a plant: that it starts from nothing and ends in nothing . . .

EWS: From silence to silence . . .

DB: From silence to silence, and that you can't stop until the end. In our technologically advanced time, it is very easy to forget what this "one timeness" is because everything can be saved and repeated through technology, whereas this cannot. You can make a tape or you can make a recording of a live concert and keep it, but for the people who are there at the concert, it never comes again.

EWS: Yes, I think this is something that seems very problematic to me because, with both literature and painting, time isn't always going forward: one can go around, come back, read, re-read. In other words, the occasion isn't quite as powerful as the performance, which dictates, as you said, the logic of going forward from beginning to end. A performance has no repeatability in a way. Even if there is a tape, it's not the same thing; it's already another. Don't you think?

DB: Of course, even if it is repeated the next day, it is a different performance.

EWS: And so the question is: Does the element of waste and loss come into it, so that there's a certain built-in undercutting of the music by silence, which, in literature, we preserve? All of the readings and re-readings, in the case of some writers, can theoretically be included in the text—somebody who wants to keep coming back to change during the process of editing, and so on. And even for the critic, there's the opportunity to read and re-read constantly all that's preserved in print. For the musician, that sense of loss, when the performance is over and silence is restored, reminds me, for example, of the way, in some of the Beethoven middle period works, like the Fifth Symphony or the end of *Fidelio,* there's almost a kind of hysteria to affirm something at the end. Like a great C-major throbbing, which is an attempt to forestall, defer, evade the ending.

DB: As if to defy silence . . .

EWS: As a way of defying silence and prolonging the sound. Do you see that?

DB: I see that very well. But I see music, in many ways, as a defiance of physical laws—one of them is the relation to silence. The main difference between a Beethoven symphony and the sonnets of Shakespeare is that, although the words, as written in the book, are a notation of Shakespeare's thoughts —in the same way that the score is nothing but a notation of what Beethoven imagined—the difference is that the thoughts existed in Shakespeare's mind and in the reader's mind. But in the Beethoven symphonies, there is the added element of actually bringing these sounds into the world: in other words, the sounds of the Fifth Symphony do not exist in the score.

That is the phenomenology of sound—the fact that sound is ephemeral, that sound has a very concrete relation to silence. I often compare it to the law of gravity; in the same way that objects are drawn to the ground, so are sounds drawn to silence, and vice versa. And if you accept that, then you have a whole dimension of physical inevitabilities, which as a musician you try to defy. This is why courage is an integral part of making music. Beethoven was courageous not only because he was deaf but also because he had to overcome superhuman challenges. The sheer act of making music is an act of courage since you are trying to defy many of the physical laws of nature. The first one is a question of silence. If you want to maintain the sound and if you want to create the tension that comes from sustained sound, the first moment of relationship is between the first sound and the silence that precedes it, and the next one is between the first and the second note, and so on ad infinitum. In order to achieve this, you are defying the law of nature; you're not letting the sound die as it naturally would tend to. And therefore, in the performance, besides knowing the music and understanding it, the first important thing for a musician to understand is how does sound operate when you bring it into this world, when you bring it into this room. In other words, what is the reverberation? What is the prolongation of the sound? And the art of making music through sound is, for me, the art of illusion. You create, on the piano, the illusion of being able to let the sound grow on one note, which the piano is totally incapable of doing, physically. You defy that. You create the illusion through the phrasing, through the use of the pedal, through many ways. You create the illusion of growth of a tone, which doesn't exist, and you can also create the illusion of slowing down the process of decreasing volume. And I think, with the orchestra, it's different because some of the instruments can sustain it. But the art of illusion, and the art of defying physical laws, is the first element that strikes me in a performance. And this is what one has to prepare and rehearse—not, however, to arrive at a formula for performance, which is, unfortunately, in my opinion, very often the case.

EWS: You mean a gimmick of some sort?

DB: No, not necessarily a gimmick; a formula in the sense of arriving at certain conclusions about balance, about tempo, and about phrasing, and being satisfied with what one has arrived at, having corrected what one dislikes in order simply to try and achieve that again in the evening as a performance. This is, for me, a total misunderstanding.

EWS: Isn't it the case that performers, like all interpreters, are people who have a particular style with regard to the text that they are trying to enact? So, when I read, let's say, a play by Shakespeare and then a novel by Dickens, they are totally different kinds of works. One was written in the sixteenth or early seventeenth century, and the other was written in the middle or later part of the nineteenth century. And yet, I am the same person reading them. And so, I'm conscious of a certain set of interests that I bring, as reader, which would not necessarily be the same as those of another reader. So, I notice a certain continuity in my own style of reading, which extends through the works that I read and try to interpret. For me, it seems that one of the things that one doesn't want to do is to be predictable and have it said, "Well, this is, for instance, a mythic reading of *The Tempest,* and Said, as usual, is doing a mythic reading of *Great Expectations,* a novel by Dickens." On the other hand, I think that what one wants is, nevertheless, to have a distinctive style of one's own, no matter what one is reading. In other words, whether it's Shakespeare or Dickens or Pope, there is a recognizable intelligence and personality doing the interpreting that one wants to preserve. So, the balance, then—and I think that's what you were saying about the formula—is between a distinctive though characteristic style and total predictability. In other words, one doesn't want to go in and just do the same thing over and over again, but one wants to make certain that people understand that this performance or this interpretation is yours and not somebody else's.

DB: Well, I wasn't quite thinking so much in that line. I was thinking of the difference in rehearsal and performance more along the lines of using the rehearsal to make sure that what one considers wrong, whether in phrasing or accentuation, does not happen in the performance. In other words, you can't put everything into alcohol and preserve it so that, in the evening, you open the bottle and it is there. And I think that the examination and observation of the phenomenology of sound is extremely important in rehearsal, and especially in an orchestra. It's also true for a solo piece, but in an orchestral situation, it's easier to see what I mean. After all, the composer's notation is, in some respects, much more approximate than people like to think—you know, this question of truthful to the letter, it doesn't really exist.

EWS: Why?

DB: Because the score is not the truth. The score is not the piece. The piece is when you actually bring it into sound.

EWS: So, you don't think there's an absolute object called the piece?

33

DB: No, no.

EWS: There's a school of criticism that says there is no stable textual object and that every object is created anew in the reading or performance or interpretation of it. What is a troubling thing, then, is the notation of a score or text—let's call it a text, because that's what it is; I mean, we're talking about a printed object. Where would one set the minimum of what is required to produce the performance? There is extreme literalness, or fundamentalism, where you say, "Well, he says this; therefore, we have to do it just that way."

DB: The audibility of a score. In other words, when Beethoven writes *crescendo,* he doesn't write *crescendo* at one point for the flutes and then two bars later for the clarinets and then the strings and then one bar before the *forte* for the trumpets and timpani.

EWS: No. It's all together.

DB: Exactly. If you let all these instruments do the *crescendo* at one time, by the second bar you don't hear anything. Obviously, the timpani and the trumpets will cover everybody else. The second flute doesn't stand a chance with that. Therefore, you start, already, with a very simple question of balance, of audibility, without getting into questions of interpretation. I don't think the word "interpretation" comes into all of this. Audibility. Transparency. How do you create it? The minute you make it audible, are you being truthful to the text by asking the trumpets and the timpani to start the *crescendo* considerably later and to give the last impulse before the climax? In a way, you are being unfaithful to the text because you're actually changing it. It's a very small example. I'm only saying this to try and make clear the approximate nature of the musical notation. A note is a note. That's clear. But that's where it ends, even when it says that there's a dynamic indication— *forte,* that means loud, yes, but in relation to what? And this is what I mean by the observation of the phenomenology of sound: how the sound accumulates; how you can create the illusion of a sound being longer than you wanted; how you can create the illusion of sound starting out of nowhere—an objective impossibility and, yet, the very essence of making music. When you hear a Bruckner symphony with the string *tremolos* starting out of nowhere, this is a creation of illusion because if you measure it purely physically, you know, at one point, the sound starts. At the beginning *tremolo* of the Bruckner Fourth or Seventh Symphony, you create the illusion that it starts out of nowhere and that sound creeps out of silence, like some beast coming out of the sea and making itself felt before it is seen. This may sound very poetic or metaphysical, but it is a defiance. In order to defy a physical law, you have to understand that physical law and to understand how it is that things sound in a certain way and why. And from there, you go to the question of phrasing, and even that has to do with the question of time and space. In tonal music how much time is required for a chord that has a very important function of creating, or having created, tension to achieve the release of that tension? In other words, there is a certain amount of time necessary for that. And this, to my mind, is what has to be rehearsed. This is what the purpose of the rehearsal is, taking into account that the orchestra already knows the notes, that it already knows how to play, that it already knows what kind of sound one wants, and all that. Basically, when you stand in front of a great orchestra like the Chicago Symphony or the

Berlin Philharmonic or the Vienna Philharmonic—an orchestra that knows the repertoire inside out—it is precisely that: the creation of a set of totally undisputed conceptions of the sound relations, which is basically what, then, allows you to make music. This is what differentiates making music from just the production of unrelated sound. It is this organic element. And then, you have the moment of a performance. Once you have observed all of these things, and you know that a certain *crescendo* doesn't have to go above a certain level because there's yet another one coming two bars later and another one two pages later, and you know that the tempo has to do certain things, and that with a slight modification of tempo, which is not only accepted but actually required for the *melos* of the music to come through—when you do all that, then you are at the moment of the performance. It's not just the excitement of the fact that it's being done in public, it is not the excitement of the applause before and afterwards; and it's certainly not the excitement of getting dressed in a special way to walk on the stage. It is completely the excitement of actually being able to live a certain piece from beginning to end without any interruption, without getting out of it. In a way, for me, there's nothing comparable to that in life.

EWS: That's a very compelling description of the experience. It's an experience, really, of a kind of immediacy that is all-consuming. And one of the things that has always bothered me about the performance situation is that it's entirely a function of a modern concert hall, which is a late development in the history of music. If you go back to the period of Bach, it was very different. Bach, from all the evidence we have, of course, was a consummate technician. He was the greatest master of counterpoint, he played the organ, and he wrote music with enormous virtuosity—all informed by a kind of religious impulse to glorify God. And in the case of Beethoven and Haydn, there's a certain sense in which what they're doing is, in some direct way, aimed at their aristocratic patrons. By the time you get to composers like Brahms, what he does in the concert hall is much less concerned with an audience or an institution like the church, and it's much more about music internally. What you can see is a kind of gradual self-sufficiency of music and of the performing occasion—at a remove from the patrons and even the audience. I once called performance an extreme occasion—that is to say, it's removed from the other pursuits of life, whether we call them religious or philosophical, and so on. I'm very interested whether, for the performer, there's that sense—that you are able to concentrate only on this particular sound world that you're creating.

DB: I agree entirely with everything you said except maybe with one small thing. I think that, already in Mozart, and certainly in Beethoven, there is a self-sufficiency there, as well as a preoccupation with the aristocracy.

EWS: Oh yes, there is. And there is in Bach, too. One can see the self-sufficiency in the late works, like the *Art of Fugue*. Who's he writing that for?

DB: Yes, but I think that this is a very important parallel with the social and political development of the society in that time. Bach's music was written, in many ways, for the glory of God and, as such, uses epic means. A fugue becomes a real construction of a musical building, stone upon building stone, level upon level, for the glory of God or for the church. And then, if you start looking at Haydn and Mozart, you find that

37

revolution is in the air. This is applied by different formal means: sonata form, with already contrasting elements, whether you want to call it masculine and feminine, active and contemplative. You're already dealing with elements that are put in juxtaposition and in conflict with each other.

EWS: And the same in Beethoven . . .

DB: Even more so, but still, with a certain belief in the overall positive nature of life. In other words, it is not coincidence that the funeral march in the *Eroica* is the second movement and not the last movement. I think, for me, there's a symbol in that: to say that grief is also something transitional.

EWS: In other words, you have to go through it to get to the affirmation.

DB: In Beethoven, very much so. And then, in the development after late Beethoven and late Schubert, you get into Brahms, and Berlioz, Liszt, and Wagner—the so-called Romantic style with a much greater dose of chromaticism, until finally there's Wagner's *Tristan,* which is at an extreme of tonal writing.

EWS: In Wagner, one of the things that has always struck me as very compelling and, at the same time, bizarre is a kind of extreme reaction to the loss of a world that he can rely on in some way. Let's just call it an outside world, a world of men and women and habits and institutions, and so on. In other words, even with Beethoven, who's such a revolutionary, who makes such a tremendous play out of contrasts—the drama of contrasts, which you mentioned, for example, in the *Eroica*—

there is a sense that he can rely on a world in which all this is taking place. One gets the sense that it's taking place somewhere actual. The thing that has always struck me as quite extraordinary about Wagner (and also the parallel development in the late nineteenth century of the huge novel by Balzac or Dickens) is the feeling that you can no longer rely on the world, but you have to make your own world. For me, the most extraordinary moment in Wagner is the beginning of *Rheingold* where, with the long series of sustained E-flats, he wants to give you the illusion that the world is being born, and he's making it come alive. And that creates, for me, a sense of isolation; that is to say, the artistic world or the aural world of Wagner is very special to Wagner precisely because it's so hermetic.

DB: Yes, but I think all progress is, in fact, having the courage to do away with the support of the past. Look at the switch from Bach, on the one hand, to Haydn, Mozart, Beethoven, on the other hand, and then from Haydn, Mozart, Beethoven to Wagner. You could say that you could rely on God in Bach's time, and in Beethoven's time, you couldn't rely on God anymore. You had to rely on mere mortals. And Wagner says you can't even do that; we have to create a new kind of human being.

EWS: And, of course, there's a certain extent to which he thinks of himself as the human being. I mean, there's an element of Siegfried in him. You know, when Siegfried, in the opera of that name, forges the sword, Wagner's doing the same thing. But what I'm trying to say is that Wagner has to begin with the fragments, and the fragments are partially inherited from somewhere else. But what he wants to convince you of is that he has made it all from scratch. And that particular kind of illusion—you know, that I'm really beginning from the beginning, and I don't need anything else—leads to what, to me, is a very troubling thing, which is the isolation of music from the social and cultural world. In other words, here's a sense of intellectual and aesthetic isolation that requires much more effort, for example, than somebody like Bach, who's writing in the security of the church, in the security of society in which there's no challenge. You don't feel from Bach a sense of challenge to the authorities. In *Meistersinger,* for example, Wagner is trying to create a new Germany, given the fragmented state of the country. In other words, it's much more ambitious.

DB: Yes. But to be fair, I don't think it is quite precise to compare an opera—especially an opera with Wagner's ideas and development of ideas—with absolute music or most cantatas.

EWS: No, but one can't imagine Wagner writing a B minor Mass. You see, I'm talking about even that. There's a kind of set procedure for the mass, which Bach, of course, makes more personal. But if you compare Bach's B minor Mass and, say, Beethoven's *Missa solemnis,* there's already quite a big difference. The *Missa solemnis* is a very strange work, in a way —of course, it's a very late work. But you don't get the impression that Beethoven has the full confidence that Bach has in the material, religious and aesthetic.

DB: This is the difference between the eighteenth and nineteenth centuries. It is a great paradox that music can really have its fullest force of intensity and expression if it is isolated in a room or in a concert hall. The actual element of isolating music from the rest of the universe is extremely important because, in a way, it is the creation of a sound universe. If a listener is able and willing to attach himself, as it were, to the first note in a performance and really stay attached, without any wavering of concentration, to the end, he has actually lived through a whole universe, whether it is a short work of Chopin or a huge symphony of Bruckner. On the one hand, music exists in isolation and, on the other, it mirrors or often anticipates social development. There was the certitude of the church and how people believed blindly, in many ways, in the eighteenth century. Then, there comes the revolutionary spirit that starts in Haydn, Mozart, and Beethoven, where there is much more chromaticism, where there are the form changes. The sonata form is a form of tension, of strife, and of development, but still with a positive outlook—with a belief in the healthiness of the society and the humanitarian ideas. All that breaks apart by the time we get to Wagner and, as you said, Balzac and Dickens in literature. Suddenly, the sonata form doesn't really give composers the basis for the expression that it did up to Brahms. And therefore, Liszt and Strauss invent the tone poem; Wagner creates his music dramas. The hierarchy of tonality—which accepted the greater importance of certain chords—is beginning to be dissected and suddenly undermined. In other words, it's not the hierarchy of God anymore. There's not even the hierarchy of the social classes in the kingdom. Now, you have a republic, with tonic, dominant, subdominant, and all these musical terminologies, which show order and hierarchy, until you end with the atonality, where all twelve tones are equal.

EWS: I'm one of the people who actually believes what Theodor Adorno says about this passage that you've just described. That is to say, what you're really moving from is a kind of music that is written for society, in the case of the earlier composers, such as Bach, but also Beethoven. There's a compact between Beethoven and his listeners, which is always being challenged by Beethoven's peculiar excesses and extra drama, which is what makes him so extraordinary a composer. Adorno says when you get to people like Schoenberg, however, where all the tones are equal, you get to a point where it becomes very difficult to listen to the music. And in fact, Adorno actually says that music of that sort is really not to be listened to. It can't be heard, in a way, because it's almost too much of an effort to understand the totally atomized and organized sound world of a twelve-tone work. There isn't the sense of the drama and the contrasts, which you have, let's say, in a Beethoven sonata, nor is there the drama, the development, the affirmations, and, in the end, the negations, let's say, as in the Wagner. So, I just wondered, when you perform Schoenberg, do you feel that there's more isolation and more removal in what you're doing than, let's say, there would be if you were playing Liszt or Bach?

DB: I still think the greatest sense of isolation and removal from anything, for me—but this is very subjective, and I do not claim this to be objective—is in late Beethoven. If you look at the *Grosse Fuge,* you look at passages of the *Missa solemnis,* and you look at the Diabelli Variations or the last three piano sonatas, this is total isolation and removal from the world, much more so than Schoenberg.

EWS: I heard you playing Schoenberg in a recital several years ago, where there was an almost romantic yearning and a sense of quite passionate searching; whereas in the late Beethoven that you are talking about, what is very powerful and, as you described it, extremely desolate is that there's something irreconcilable about it, in some way. In other words, instead of get-

42

ting resolutions, you're getting things being pulled apart. Isn't that what you feel?

DB: Yes. But I think you are referring to a concert where I played Opus 11 of Schoenberg, which are relatively early pieces and, therefore, have a certain expressionistic yearning.

EWS: Right.

DB: But I think that the elements of building up and release of harmonic tension, so essential in the tonal system, are largely gone with the twelve-tone. There's no question about that. On the other hand, I find accumulation very strong in twelve-tone music, the kind that you get in Bruckner: huge *crescendos,* when the sequences are repeated one on top of the other, sometimes with total lack of harmonic progression, where you only get repetition of the motives with ever-increasing tension and volume. The expressivity of accumulation is very strong, for me, in Schoenberg and in Berg.

EWS: But not in Webern. Webern is almost performing a dissection and x-ray analysis of his contemporaries, in a way, like a reaction to what you're saying.

DB: I'm not convinced that the tonal system is a pure and simple fabrication of man, nor am I convinced that it is a law of nature. I vacillate from one to the other.

EWS: You mean in its origin?

DB: Yes, and in its existence, too. And I think that sometimes, in Schoenberg, when you have the twelve tones with their search for equality and denial of the hierarchy of tonality, this cannot fight a certain element of order that the ear has developed and that yearns for some kind of tonal consonance. And the dissonance, taken to the extreme, as it is sometimes in Schoenberg, produces some kind of consonance, which is probably totally unwanted by the composer. And the difficulty with listening to a lot of the Second Viennese School has to do with lack of familiarity for the listener. I think that if you listen over and over again, it is obviously more complex than a simple Haydn symphony. With a Haydn symphony, you remember the tunes much more easily; you remember certain rhythmic patterns. The Schoenberg Opus 16 pieces take, obviously, much more effort to understand and to absorb; but once you do that, I think that the element of tension and release of tension is gone, or diminished, but the element of accumulation as an expression is even stronger. And then you have to ask yourself: does music have a purpose, a social purpose, and what is it? Is it to provide comfort and entertainment, or is it to ask disturbing questions of the performer and of the listener? If you look at the role that music, and much more than music—theater and opera—played in societies and the totalitarian regimes, it was the only place that political ideas and social totalitarianism could be criticized. In other words, a performance of Beethoven, under the Nazis or under any kind of totalitarian regime, whether left or right, suddenly assumes the call for freedom, even becomes a very direct criticism of the policies of the regime and, therefore, is actually a much more disturbing and, at the same time, uplifting thing. This is a long way from the entertainment of Mozart divertimentos or Johann Strauss waltzes.

EWS: There's the argument that literature is more interesting when produced in a situation where there's extreme censorship, so that one pays close attention to all kinds of ingenuities and subterfuges that the writer uses. For me, what is troubling is that in a society like ours where art and music are part of the luxury of routine—for example, there's a symphony subscription, and on a given day, the Chicago Orchestra is going to play the Beethoven and the Brahms symphonies: how can one determine what the purpose of music is in a context like that? Is it to confirm—to confirm the existent situation, since there's no need for it to challenge? You're not criticizing in the same way as you would in a society, such as the one you mentioned, where the nine Beethoven symphonies or *Fidelio* stand as a kind of affirmation of freedom which is otherwise unavailable. In a society in which there is a kind of accepted threshold of freedom, such as this one, then what do these works signify? Are they merely confirmation of the status quo? Do they confirm the power and attractiveness of the institution of the orchestra, which becomes a kind of symbol of the prosperity of the society? As an intellectual, I feel that I'm not interested in finding that out over and over. What I'm interested in doing is always to challenge what is given. What would be the parallel in music, in the performance of music? I wonder whether it's possible.

DB: Yes. I think so. Let's stay, for the sake of argument, with the example of Beethoven, and let's remove ourselves from *Fidelio,* which has ideas and which has text. Let's stay with absolute music. What role can the *Eroica* Symphony play today? You do not play the *Eroica* Symphony just because it is a very famous piece and it guarantees that more people will buy tickets and come to hear the concert. The *Eroica* was not necessarily thought of as a critique of society or a regime; nor was it written for the glory of the French Revolution, and all that. I think that there is a very important personal message in each one of these Beethoven pieces. In other words, yes, in the West, we have, as you rightly say, an acceptably livable amount of freedom, but how free is the human being? How does the human being deal with himself? How does he deal with his problems of existence? How does he deal with problems of his place in society? How does he see himself? How does he cope with his anxieties, with anguish? How does he cope with joy? How does he cope with all those things? All that, and much more, is, for me, the substance of a Beethoven symphony. There is a parallel, hundreds of parallels. For instance, if we again look at the Beethoven Fourth Symphony from a purely harmonic point of view, the introduction is a search for tonality. It begins with a lone B-flat. It could be B-flat. It could be A-sharp. It could be in any kind of tonality. And then, the strings move, as in unison, without giving you any idea of the tonality. Then, at the end of this introduction, you are basically in the dominant chord of B-flat that the piece began with, except when it started it was not clear whether it was going to be major or minor. And then, the main *Allegro* of the piece, the whole exposition, with its two themes, is an affirmation of B-flat. What is the purpose of establishing that? The purpose is to establish a very secure sense of home tonality. In other words, B-flat has become the home of the music. Then, through a very astute enharmonic change—in other words, when B-flat and A-sharp become the same note—we suddenly get into totally foreign territory at the end of the development section. Why is it foreign? Because home has already been established. And this is what I would call the psychology of tonality. This is creating a sense of home, going to an unknown territory, and then returning. This is a process of courage and inevitability. There is the affirmation of the key—you want to call it the affirmation of self, the comfort of the known territory—in order to be able to go somewhere totally unknown and have the courage to get lost and, then, find again this famous dominant, in an unexpected way, that leads us back home. Isn't that a sort of parallel of the process that every human being has to go through in his inner life in order to first achieve the affirmation of what one is, then have the courage to let that identity go in order to find the way back. I think this is what music is about. I wouldn't say that it is always a criticism of society or of the human being, but it *is* a parallel of the inner process of the innermost thoughts and feelings of a human being. I think this is what Beethoven is about. I don't know whether I've convinced you.

EWS: No, I think it's convincing. What you've described is an allegory that corresponds to one of the great myths that we find in literature, which is the myth of home, discovery, and return: the odyssey. There is absolutely a parallel between the explorations of Beethoven and of Homer, but having both the courage to leave and then to return is not just wandering away and coming back; there's a certain working out that is extremely intricate. Odysseus leaves home, leaves Penelope and his comforts in Ithaca. He goes to war and returns when it is over. But it's not just returning—that's where the fantastic power of the *Odyssey* is—but returning through one series of adventures after another, to which he's attracted. He could have just come home. But he is also a curious man. It's not just a matter of leaving home, it's leaving home and discovering things that attract you as well as threaten you. That's the point. He could have avoided his adventure with Polyphemus, the great one-eyed giant. But he felt he had to talk to him, he had to have a direct experience of challenging the fearsome creature, in order to finally return home, via these kinds of adventures, which is not the same as simply coming home after a day at the office.

DB: Of course. That is the same thing in the sonata form. The recapitulation is not the same as the exposition, although the notes are the same.

EWS: Yes, exactly. So there's that sense in which, even at home, when he comes back to it, there's an interference. It's a different kind of place. It could be richer. There's a threat in it, perhaps. It's a slightly more complex thing, as Cavafy observes. So it's not the solid return where everything ends. It's the return where you feel that something new could begin. So, that's one kind of very powerful experience. We find another in the *Iliad*, which is that of wandering and homelessness. In other words, these are people—the Greeks, I mean, since Homer concentrates on them—who are far away from home, many of whom, like Achilles, are going to die; they're not going to come home. In other words, there's no return here but a profound, unending finality. So, this is an experience not so much only of desolation—it's not desolation—it's really an experience of extraordinary adventure, but constant experience of death as well.

DB: Masada.

EWS: But, in Masada, for example, there's a kind of purposefulness: we don't want to be killed by the Romans. But in the case of the *Iliad,* there's a certain sense in which Homer is really talking about a pure death-like force. There's a kind of senselessness to it. This is a war that's been going on for ten years. What's the point of it? Combatants have forgotten the original cause almost completely. And there's a certain exercise of arms, the martial spirit, and a kind of recklessness, which has no purpose, in the end, except combat itself. I wonder whether there's a parallel for that in music, where in the Second Viennese School, the absence of tonality is a kind of homelessness, a kind of permanent exile because you're not going to come back. And I think the typology exists in human experience.

DB: You mean the Second Viennese School as refugees' music?

EWS: Yes. Exiles' music—not only from the social world but also from the tonal world, if the tonal world by the time they inherit it is the accepted world, the world of habit and custom and a certain kind of solidity.

DB: I hadn't thought about it in this sense, but it's very convincing to me the way you put it.

EWS: What you have also, in the modernist literature of the period, is a sense of trying to recover and being unable to do so, in the works of, let's say, Proust, Joyce, Eliot, and others.

DB: There is a limit to these associations, using a specific terminology Words such as redemption, glory, or revolution, whatever it is, bring with them the danger of then using the music, even on a subconscious level, as a description of these ideas. I think that the true expression of absolute music has to be found in the world of sound and sound relations themselves. And then, the listener will be able to adapt that to whatever situation he is in, whether it is a situation of comfort, whether it is a situation of homelessness, a situation of strife.

EWS: You don't, as a performer, have those kinds of images going through your head?

DB: I don't. I have no images whatsoever. Even in Wagner. Of course, I have studied the text and analyzed the ideas that come from the text; but I always try to find the true expression of it in the music on its own—and very often, if I find what, to me, seems to be the true sense of the music, it goes hand in hand with the text; and if it doesn't, then the text suddenly doesn't fit, and then something is wrong. But I don't believe in studying the text first and then trying to see how the music fits because, although Wagner wrote the libretto first and then the music, he was looking for an art form that unified them. And he made a unity of sound and words going absolutely and indivisibly hand in hand. And the expression doesn't come only from the fact that there are very important sentiments expressed, whether it is love, death, or whatever it is, but it occurs almost onomatopoeically, when somehow the sound of the syllable, joined with a certain sound that comes in the music, is already part of the expression. And I think that if one studies the text first and then sees how the music matches, of course, it will match, because it was meant to, but then you don't get the same depth of musical expression as when you try to study that separately. I think one has to study the musical text and the literary text totally independently and, then, see how they fit together. But you diminish the capacity of expression if you try to adapt the music to your analysis of the text. This is why I don't use images, although it can be sometimes very entertaining to use images. I think it was Karajan who said that there're only six things that you should tell the orchestra: too loud; too soft; too late; too soon; too fast; too slow. Of course, this has to be the result of having digested the total content of the piece in order to do that.

EWS: There is another parallel between what you play and conduct and what I write about and lecture on. A lot of what we do is based in the nineteenth century, but we are twentieth- and twenty-first-century people. When I'm writing and lecturing about the works of the past, my main interest is to try to explain them and present them, as much as possible, as creations of their time. For me, a Jane Austen novel or Verdi's *Aida* are very much located, in Austen's case, in the early nineteenth century, and the other in the late nineteenth century, and my reading of them tries, as much as possible, to take that into account. In other words, I can't expect of Jane Austen that she be like Proust. Obviously, there are certain things that she can do that Proust wouldn't think of doing or couldn't possibly do; and the same with Verdi in *Aida*, where there's a certain expectation about the nature of opera and its audience, which is unique to his time. But I wonder, very often, because of my interest in the past, whether I'm too much in the past. When you're conducting and playing, you're not really always concerned, principally, with playing the works of your time, although one does that. You certainly commission and play works by contemporary composers. But the main staple of your diet, as for me, is the great work of the past. So, then, a question of relevance comes up. How much do you feel that you're distorting works from the past in order to put them, let's say, in the context of a brilliant late-twentieth-century orchestra like the Chicago Symphony? When you take a work, let's say a Beethoven symphony, composed for a particular location—a much smaller orchestra and space—and transform it for the twentieth century, it somewhat violates the past. Do you feel, as I do, that there's a kind of constant going back and forth between the requirements of the past and the question of relevance in the present?

DB: Yes, of course, there is. But I think that every great work of art has two faces: one toward its own time and one toward eternity. In other words, there are certain aspects of a Mozart symphony or a Mozart opera that are clearly linked to their time and they have no relevance today. The *droit du seigneur* of the count in *Figaro* is so totally time-bound. But there is something that is timeless about this music, and that aspect of it has to be performed with a sense of discovery.

EWS: But why call it timeless? You're in time, you're not out of time. . . . So it can be brought up to date, in a way—that's what you're saying.

DB: Timeless in the sense that it is not only limited to that time, it is permanently contemporary. This does not apply to every piece. I don't think *Aida* is permanently contemporary, but late Beethoven certainly is. A lot of Debussy is. I think it is there that one comes into a question of taste and subjectivity. By the same token, I can mention three composers that I have performed with regularity—I would say with alarming regularity for some of our subscribers of the Chicago Symphony— Pierre Boulez, Harrison Birtwistle, and Elliott Carter: three contemporary composers.

EWS: Difficult composers.

DB: Difficult composers, and, as I said, I've played them with "alarming" regularity because I believe in the understanding of difficult situations, difficult music, or any kind of difficulties, through familiarity. Familiarity, in this case, does not breed contempt, but breeds understanding.

EWS: You don't think it takes the edge off it?

DB: Not at all. I think that one should be able to play Mozart and Beethoven with the greatest sense of discovery and of the unexpected. In other words, you have to be able to bring the listener so immediately into the piece that he, then, makes the journey, although he knows what is coming. You have to be able to make him forget that he knows.

EWS: Almost like a great actor in a part. You know what's going to happen in *Hamlet,* but what you do is relive it, in fact. That's it, isn't it?

DB: And by the same token—or rather paradoxically—to play Boulez and Carter and Birtwistle with a feeling of "self-understood" as you would play a Haydn and Mozart symphony. And I think that this is possible. But the first important quality in the performance of new music is clarity: the audibility; the transparency of the textures; and the real working out of the dynamic relations, since we are not talking about harmony here; about all the elements of expression that are in music. Why does a short note have a different expression from a long note? I think that also can be explained through the relation between sound and silence. And the short note is, in a way, a quick death, in a very simple metaphorical way. And a long note is a defiance of death; and there's a sort of yearning for perpetuity and a fight against the fluidity of life, of nature, whatever you want to call it. But, you very rarely get this sense of clarity in first performances or the performance of very difficult music. And in this respect, I think that Pierre Boulez has

been a very important figure in the second half of the twentieth century, in that he made the work of the Second Viennese
School audible with utmost clarity. And it has nothing to do
with intellectual, cold, analytical attitude. If you compare a
good performance of Schoenberg and Berg, where there is all
this clarity, with some of the performances that are done in a
very generalized way, then you see that it is impossible to understand. And I think the greatness of a performing musician
is directly tied to his preoccupation with detail. The difficulty
is to treat each detail as if it were the most important element
and yet, not lose sight of the whole piece. It's very easy to do
one or the other, but really combining the two is not easy.
When you are talking about works of the complexity of Carter,
for instance, this is particularly tricky. And the orchestral musicians do not find it easy to understand either. And this can
be achieved only by repeating a piece in a season: certain
works are played on a regular basis, and by the seventh or
eighth time, the listener is also able to hear it. And the orchestra will play them all differently. We played *Exody* by Harrison
Birtwistle in Chicago. This is a very long, complex work, and
some people in the audience left because they found it simply
too difficult and too disturbing, but the orchestra played it extremely well. It was well rehearsed, and we played it three or
four times in January 1998. We then let it rest. We took it up
again in September to play it at the Proms in London. And of
course, we took it over from where we had left it in January. In
other words, we already had an accumulation. And I can't
even say whether the performances in September were better
or not, but there was a familiarity, which means that you have
the ability to compare, you have something that you have already gone through. And therefore, the orchestra plays it in a
different way a second or a third time round. And this is very
important. For me, the idea is to play Mozart and Beethoven

as if it were a first performance—a recently commissioned piece—and to play works of Boulez and Carter as if they had already the experience of a hundred years.

EWS: They have a history, whereas in fact, they really are new pieces and of our time. I find a parallel experience for the reader and writer of literature, where a work that is very difficult—let's say, a poem by Gerard Manley Hopkins, or a novel by Joseph Conrad—can be read, but there's always something elusive about it. You never really completely pin it down. But for me, the idea would be in reading and presenting it to get myself finally in the position of the author writing it. In other words, it's not as if there's the work and you're just repeating it; but rather that by reading in a specially alternative way you're producing the work in a new form. I mean, this is the sense that you have, so that you can have a kind of familiarity with the work, where you feel you're at the point of origin of the work and proceeding with it as it unfolds. So, there's a certain kind of identification, which I think is possible in music as well, where, in conducting and performing, you're not just conducting it and performing it. And one can tell that right away in a performance. You know immediately when something is being done from the outside. There's a wonderful expression where we say, "He's inward with it"; in other words, that you and the piece are at the same point of unfolding and disclosure. And obviously, there's a certain amount of technical preparing, rehearsing, which is part of the experience of the performer, the musician, the interpreter. But what you have to be able to do is to get beyond all of that and live the piece in its own terms at the same time that you are, in fact, presenting it as yours. And the question is: how much distortion is allowed, and how much freedom does one have? I think it's always a question of fidelity in some way. As the person who's performing something new or something that isn't yours, you feel a certain sense of loyalty and fidelity to that work, but also, you have to have that sense of fidelity to yourself, as the interpreter. In other words, this is your particular way of doing it, and you want to convince others that this is the way. And the ultimate test of the persuasiveness of what you're doing is that it sounds as if it is being composed and staged at that very moment.

DB: Of course.

EWS: And, in a certain sense, you as a performer playing Carter are also the same Daniel Barenboim who has played Beethoven and Bach and Wagner, so that whole history, as it were, is compressed into the performance of the piece. And similarly, as a reader or writer or teacher or critic, what I feel is that when I'm reading a contemporary work, say a play by Beckett, I've also read Shakespeare and all these other earlier plays, but also somehow forcing them into a kind of service of the contemporary work that's being performed in front of an audience as if for the first time.

DB: Of course. But we mustn't forget that Carter also knows his Wagner and Mozart and Debussy and his music would not be possible without that knowledge. But I think that, in the end, it is false modesty to say, as a performing musician, "I am the servant of the music. My only interest is fidelity. All I want to do is play the music exactly as it is in the score." It is either a very great arrogance, or false modesty, because it is an objective impossibility. The score is not the piece.

EWS: No, no, but what I'm trying to say is that the arrogance is required to say, "Well, that's his piece, but I'm doing it now."

You understand what I'm trying to say: there's a certain sovereignty, which one has.

DB: But I think that unless you are able to digest the piece to the point where you feel it is part of you, even though it may be incomplete, then you shouldn't perform it. I think at the moment that you do it, you have to have the feeling that you and it are inseparable. The trouble is, when one speaks about freedom in today's critical world, this applies almost exclusively to freedom of speed, freedom of tempo. When somebody says in criticism of performances, "He was free with the tempo"; or "He was very strict," it implies "He was strict, therefore he's analytical, uncompromising"; "He was free with the tempo, therefore he's romantic, emotional."

EWS: That's stupid.

DB: Of course it is. But this is also part of the mentality of our age—that everything is made compact, reduced to a token or a slogan. There is a contradiction in the fact that we live in an age that considers itself extremely critical but does not require of the individual to have the means to criticize.

EWS: Or the culture, which requires a lot of effort, a lot of patience.

DB: I read once somewhere that Chomsky refuses to speak on television because he knows that he will not be given the time to explain a concept to the end, and I have a lot of respect for that.

EWS: Yes, and I've stopped doing that too. I used to do a lot of media appearances. You have to do it in what they call sound bites. I'm completely against it. I just think it's a waste of time. That's why I prefer now as a means of expression, either writing or giving a lecture, where you have time to develop ideas in front of an audience. I understand the attraction of a kind of guerrilla intervention—you do it quickly and you disturb. That's fine, but it's not enough. The person has to be actually intervening rather than dipping into a debate. A musician intervenes in the life of his audience. The audience is leaving everything else and interrupting their lives to come and listen to you. Similarly, people who want to read me have to put something aside in order to devote the time. For this intervention to be effective requires discipline on my part, and that discipline involves knowing something, having a particular culture, having a particular training. I think it's terribly important. In my case, it is what you'd call a philological training, where you read the texts in a historical context and understand the discipline of the language and its forms and its discourses; for you, the study of classical music, understanding the forms of a sonata, the variation, the symphony, or whatever. This training is beginning to disappear among the young musicians of our time. And what you have instead is a kind of, in my opinion, baseless eclecticism: "Ah! Beethoven: Da-da-da-dum." It's a phrase of that sort. Or "Beethoven is the composer who does X and Y."

DB: Well, it's a slogan. For me, there is a clear philosophical criticism of slogans, of the language of television, which is that it does not take into account the relation between content and time. In other words, certain content demands a particular amount of time, and you cannot compress it and you cannot abbreviate it. It's as if you would say: "Well, give me the essence of Beethoven's score in two minutes."

EWS: Or, as they used to have all those cheap recordings promising "the world's most popular themes," where there were extracts from pieces of music to give a kind of condensed digest of the work. That, I think, completely betrays the whole thing, much as the "soundtrack" of *Amadeus* played as a self-sufficient rendition of Mozart betrays Mozart.

DB: Completely. And I think that in every process, whether it is a cultural process or whether it is a political process, there is an absolutely innate relationship between the content and the time that it takes. And there are certain things, where if you don't give the time or if you give too much time, it dissipates. I mean, the Oslo Accord, for me, is an absolutely clear example of that, regardless of whether you were in favor or against the Oslo Accord. I know you were against it. I was hopeful that it would work. But the main reason, for me, that it didn't work is because the momentum—in other words, the speed, the tempo—of the process did not go hand in hand with the content. Maybe this is a sort of philosophical confirmation of your rejection of the process; in other words, there was something that was wrong and, therefore, it couldn't have its own tempo. But this is absolutely, for me, a parallel with playing music, where the content requires a given speed, and if you play it at the wrong speed—in other words, much too slow or much too fast, and the whole thing falls apart. This is what happened to the Oslo Accord.

EWS: But according to my way of thinking, the problem with the Oslo Accord was that it was notations—since it was texts, written down—that didn't conform adequately to the reality of the situation. In other words, it's like looking at a great range of mountains and deciding that you could represent that range of mountains on a small piece of paper by drawing only one mountain. And I think the problem with the Oslo Accord was that there was a tremendous disparity between the reality—in the case of the Palestinians, a sense of frustration, homelessness, exile, dispossession, which required redress—and a text that said, "Well, no, we're not going to talk about all that; we're just going to talk about the clothes you're wearing"—and so, that disparity between the reality and the text was what made it flawed. Add to that what you said. In other words, if it had unfolded in a particular way leading slowly to the range of mountains, that would have been one thing. But, in fact, what happened was that the range of mountains, represented by this one single mountain, went in a completely other direction, at the wrong tempo, gradually revealing itself to be more and more inadequate to the situation it was trying to remedy.

DB: But I think that these kinds of conflicts, in a way, cannot be solved by political means. I've often thought: What is the difference between a politician and an artist? A politician can only work and do good if he masters the art of compromise: tries to find the areas where the different parties are able and willing to compromise, bring them as close as possible together, and then hope that with the right momentum and the right time, it will become seamless; whereas the artist's expression is only determined by his total refusal to compromise in anything—the element of courage. And therefore, I think that a conflict of this nature will not be solved only through political means, through economical means, or through arrangements. It requires the courage of everybody to use, as it were, artistic solutions.

EWS: Yes, I know, but why do we, in some profound sense—I'm speaking for myself now—distrust and dislike politicians?

Precisely for the reason that they're fixers. They're more interested in any end rather than in a larger process. What they want to do is to get to the next position and say, "Look what I've done"; whereas for an intellectual or for an artist, the main thing is the ideal, without any compromises. You have something that you want to do, and you're not really interested in whether you could make little arrangements on the side to assure yourself of a certain kind of comfort, which is what the politician wants. And the question is: Is there any way of bridging the gap? That's a difficult question—whether the methods of the politician can be open to the methods of the artist and the intellectual?

DB: Well, in a way, this is also the difference of the politician and the statesman, isn't it? A statesman is somebody with a vision.

EWS: Somebody like Nehru or Mandela who has the vision and, at the same time, the capacity to carry it out, whatever that might involve . . .

DB: Somebody who has the ability to differentiate between what exists now and what could or should be. And in order to do that, you have to understand the reality, first of all. This phrase "politically correct" already means philosophically incorrect because it means compromising . . .

EWS: Compromising and conforming. It would be like a musician saying, "Well, I'm not going to discover Beethoven by working on the score and trying to figure it out for myself but by listening to a recording and just repeating it"; in other words, trying to take some example and just copying.

DB: The element of courage is the most important. Courage does not mean simply to play things in a different way, but the courage to be completely uncompromising: on the one hand, like a great statesman, to have understood the reality, understood the text, understood the difficulties of doing it, and then, to have the vision of really going all out with utmost courage. In other words, if you have a *crescendo* in Beethoven that goes to the end, and then there is a *subito piano* that creates the illusion of a precipice, you have to do that. You have to go to the precipice, to the end, and then not fall, and not make a *crescendo* only halfway.

EWS: What is the coward's way?

DB: Well, to make a *crescendo* only to a certain point, so that you don't get to the precipice, but you get a few meters behind it, and then you just drop to the *piano*. In other words, when Beethoven writes a *crescendo* and then *subito piano,* it means that the last note before the *subito piano* has to be the loudest note of that *crescendo*. And it takes a lot of courage to do that because it is physically difficult, sound control difficult, everything difficult, in order then to create the *subito piano*. It's much easier to take the *crescendo* only to a certain point and then let it drop so that you can comfortably lead into the *piano*. But then, the whole effect of precipice is gone. And this is what I'm talking about: courage in the act of music-making, not in what you play and where you play it. And this kind of courage, I think, is required for solving all the real profound humanitarian problems.

New York,
October 8, 1998

Chapter Three

⸻◈⸻

EWS: I've always thought that being a professional, whether it's a professional writer or professional specialist at something, is never enough. It's never quite satisfied me. One of the things that I believe, in my own case, that I do, and that perhaps distinguishes me from many of my colleagues, is that I feel I have an attitude toward what I do, which isn't very tied to questions of technique, expertise, or professionalism, to issues that are solely limited to the field of literature, but really try to go beyond into questions of the relationship between literature and society, between literature and politics, and so on. On the other hand, I very strongly believe that the classroom, where I spend most of my teaching time, is a classroom. It's not really a place for the presentation of political programs, which was very much the case during the sixties, when people felt that the university was complicit with the state—which it may very well be—but that the classroom should be turned into a kind of alternative social space, where liberation and all kinds of other political ideas were to be simulated and expounded. Now, I feel very strongly that that's not the case. Even though I feel that there's a certain privacy, or a barrier, between the university and the society, I still feel that it's possible to be an engaged intellectual and a member of the university community. In my case, my interest in politics and the public sphere is expressed through the media, through writing, through speaking, through coalitions and alliances on issues that are important to me—human rights, the Palestinian question, and so on. The thing that I've often thought about in the case of a musician is that the musician is very much wrapped up in a tonal world, especially with performance, and that performance, in a certain sense, crowds out everything else. In your case, you are involved in the institution as well—that is to say, an opera house and a symphony orchestra as an institution in a city, in a society. Is it possible to talk about the world of the musician as a social one at all? Is there any parallel between one situation and the other?

DB: I think that there is a parallel in the sense that a good teacher does not give information but educates. And I think that a lot of the trouble with the education today at schools, let alone the university, is that it provides information: everything in synopsis form, just information instead of education. And what attracted me to your books, especially *Culture and Imperialism,* is precisely that it isn't about information. The purpose of your book, as I see it, is to awaken the thinking capabilities of each reader in his own original way, so that you are pointing him in the direction he is inspired to go. And I think that for a musician, this is also true. In that respect, the main parallel is between a writer and a composer, not between a writer and a performer. And I think that because the whole level of education is very much lower today than it used to be, the schools give much more information and much less education. I think that the institutions, the great musical institutions—whether they are symphony orchestras or opera houses —will, in the twenty-first century, have to do much more with educating: educating the public and educating the young people. And I think that the greatest progress in public attitude, in the last fifty years, is that there is neither an embarrassment nor an arrogance on the part of the public and that the public openly expresses its thirst for knowledge. The best proof of that is surtitles. Fifty years ago, it would have been unthinkable to put surtitles into English at the Metropolitan Opera House or, in Berlin, from Italian to German. Everybody would say, "Well, *Bohème* we know; why do we need surtitles?" This is a very positive and important step on the part of the public, who wants to understand and is willing to be educated, and all the more reason why institutions have the duty to provide this kind of education. Because the music education is so poor and, in America, practically nonexistent, it is important to make people aware. And I think aware means not only to give them biographical information about the composer, but how a piece was written, and what it was inspired by. But the most important thing is how to explain to people what sound does and I haven't quite found out how to do that, but I am always looking for it. Why is it that there is an emotive quality to sound? In other words, how to listen: how to attach yourself to the first sound in the hope of staying with it until the end of it. This is really what fascinates me.

EWS: What we're both talking about is a process by which one's constituency, one's audience, absorbs something that's fairly difficult, whether you call it music, or whether you call it history, or literature. I'm very conscious of the fact that I went through a peculiar kind of education, which was, first of all, colonial. Until I was fifteen, I always went to schools where I felt I could not belong. They were British schools, whether it was in Palestine or in Egypt. And so, I felt a kind of distance from the teachers and a system that wasn't mine; I was very conscious of a certain alienation. And I also felt that I never really had any inspiring or brilliant teachers, perhaps because of the peculiar situation. What I found was that, in the end, I had to rely on myself. In other words, you obviously go through formal training: you start with literature, history, math, and so on, and you go from grade to grade. But I was very aware also that much of my learning was my own, in my own way, and self-acquired despite the presence of a teacher. So, there was a kind of intellectual distance that I felt from ideas that weren't mine. Maybe it's a form of arrogance, but I was very much turned off. When I came to this country in the early fifties, I went first to a boarding school, and there I was even more put off for different reasons, because it was a school run in ways that were, in the end, ideological—there was a lot of religion and patriotism. There, the system, which was very different from the British system I had been in, also made it hard for me to accept willingly the material given to me by the teacher. So, there, too, I felt I was picking and choosing. So, I think independence from one's teachers is very important. I remember once being asked, "Did you ever have any inspiring teachers?" I said, "No, I never did," and somehow it hasn't been such a loss for me. I wonder whether that's the case with you. Did you have an inspiring teacher?

DB: I had the very good fortune of having a very good teacher in my father. I learned more or less accidentally from everybody else because of my admiration for them. But I cannot call anybody else a real teacher, except Nadia Boulanger, who taught me among other things to look at structure as an emo-

tional means of expression and what was emotional as structure. I have learned a tremendous amount from many of the
musicians that I came across: I started playing in public at the
age of seven and therefore I came into contact with musicians
two or three generations older then I was and was able to learn
a lot from them. When you start conducting, you haven't developed yet a sort of repertoire of movement or choreography.

EWS: You mean a kind of visible style?

DB: Yes. I would play with, for example, the conductor Dimitri
Mitropoulos and found that the particular gesture that he
made achieved a particular sound, a specific result. But when
I was conducting a little bit later—consciously sometimes,
other times unconsciously—I would do the same gesture in
the hope that I would get the same result, if this was what I
wanted. Very often, it didn't work, but it was an extremely useful way to start conducting. And it is only little by little, with
the experience, that you are able then to distill the information
from all that and begin to find your own style.

EWS: Do you feel that there are certain things that influenced
you or imprinted you, where, at some point, you had to say,
"No, that's enough; I want to do it my own way"? I feel I'm
so anti-authoritarian that I eventually always resisted. And I
was very conscious of taking a style of reading, let's say, or a
certain intellectual attitude, but then, just as consciously saying, "Well, that's enough; I'm not going to do that; I need to
make my own."

DB: Yes. For me, it was exactly the same. But some way you
vacillate between imitation being the highest form of flattery

and the anxiety of influence that you mentioned. Basically, one vacillates between the two poles. What you are saying is the very nature of paradox, isn't it? On one hand, you take, but only because you know that you will then get rid of it.

EWS: I've never wanted disciples in my own teaching and writing, whereas there are teachers, writers, and intellectuals who are very anxious to cultivate followers. That's never been interesting for me. As a teacher, the thing I feel that I can do the best is to have my students, in a certain sense, criticize me—not exactly attack me, although many have, but to declare their independence from me and to go off on their own way. And you mentioned you felt that in reading *Culture and Imperialism*. I think a certain amount of skepticism is good—you know, that you're not absolutely 150 percent sure of what you're doing.

DB: I have the feeling that you don't want disciples because basically you're not trying to indoctrinate people. You're not giving a doctrine of thought. But you are trying to awaken the students' curiosity and to give them the means by which they can develop their own curiosity. I try to do that, in a way, every day.

EWS: But do you think, as a musician, that you have a doctrine? Is there a particular Barenboimian sort of musical outlook?

DB: The only doctrine that I have in music and in music-making is that it basically comes out of the nature of paradox: that you have to have the extremes; that you have to find a way to put the extremes together, not necessarily by diminishing the extremity of each one, but to form the art of transition.

EWS: I agree with that. In other words, one doesn't feel that it's necessary to reconcile or somehow diminish and take the edge off the extremes.

DB: You have to keep the extremes but find the link, always find the link, so that there is an organic whole.

EWS: In music, would you call that an argument or just a form? One of the things that impresses me most about Glenn Gould playing Bach is the sense that, beyond the purely aural experience, there is also a kind of argument, although you can't say what the argument is.

DB: Of course.

EWS: That something is not a doctrine. Perhaps it's an argument, in the end. It's a process being made apparent.

DB: Absolutely. I think that the worst crime that one can commit against the very nature of music is to play something mechanically. To paraphrase it in a very oversimplified way: when one plays two notes, they should tell a story. From this, actually, you get into a very large area of discussion. First of all, it applies when you play an instrument alone. It applies when you play in chamber music: if you have a quartet, sometimes the four players are telling the same story in a different way; sometimes they are having dialogue; sometimes they are having argument; and sometimes they are having conflict; and this is all part of it. But the fact that one should not play even two notes mechanically means that the whole nature of the profile of an orchestral musician is defined differently. There is nothing worse than the attitude of an orchestral musician who comes and is extremely well prepared, able to play the notes perfectly but totally without any kind of character, so that the music is, as it were, then made by the conductor. And he is, in fact, saying, "I play the notes, and you make the music." And there's nothing further from the possibility of good music than that. That's where you get, of course, again, into the definition of power. And this is a very interesting point, because the conductor is always taken as a symbol of power.

EWS: There's an essay by Adorno where he talks about *Meisterschaft* or mastery (domination) with regard to Toscanini. He says Toscanini really embodies the worst aspect of this because he's an emblem of domination, in a way, where the conductor is supposed to be a kind of ultimate authority figure, and where he radiates not so much only his interpretation of the music but his power over the music in such a way.

DB: I go even further than that. I think that's the misunderstanding: on the conductor's part, on the one hand; on the orchestral musician's, on the other; and finally on the observer's, whether he's a member of the public or a critic. In other words, all three misunderstand for the simple reason that the music itself is expressed only through sound. So, if the expression of the music is only through sound, the sound is not being produced by the conductor. The sound is being produced by each individual musician in the orchestra. The conductor can be a teacher; he can be an inspiring factor; he can be an animator; every imaginable thing and its opposite. The fact remains that the sound itself and, therefore, the determination of the expression of the music is in the players' hands. And sometimes, the players don't even see that. Very often, the conductors don't see that; and then there comes a whole malfunctioning, both musical and sociological. There was a study made not long ago where orchestral musicians had one of the highest rates of dissatisfaction with their jobs.

EWS: Why? Because of the conductor?

DB: Because they were always doing what the conductor tells them. And I think that this is a real misunderstanding of the nature of music. The first impulse has to come from the person who produces the sound, from each individual musician. Every individual musician in the orchestra should know that it is not only his duty but his luck to be able to provide the initial impulse of the sound. The conductor can organize it. The conductor can change the character. But if the conductor spends even one-fifth of his energy trying to animate the musicians, then that fifth is lacking in his ability to concentrate entirely on the music. And therefore, when one speaks about the feeling of power in the actual act of making music, the conductor has to understand what the nature of sound is: that he can change everything around it, but the actual sound, in the end, is made by the musicians. In an ideal situation, this will also keep the conductor's ego within bounds; and it will also give the individual musician in the orchestra the feeling that he is not just following orders, that he's not just an instrument for somebody else's feeling of power or determination, but that he's being very creative about it, too.

EWS: And anybody who communicates, whether a musician, or a writer, or a painter, is obviously trying to have a certain amount of power not only over the material, but over the craft itself. Ruskin says, for example, that when you look at a great work by Michelangelo, you're impressed not only with the no-

bility of the work but also with the idea of power in the work—
that is to say, that Michelangelo was able to compel stone and
create with his hands a human figure of a sort that never lets
you forget that it wasn't done by an ordinary effort. So, there's
that kind of power, as well: the power to impress and the
power to sustain attention. That's on an individual level. But
on an institutional level, in the case of the orchestra, for example, or in the school or university, there's also the power of
the teacher and of the institution, which makes students go
through a certain regime. One of the things in my work that
keeps me within bounds is the knowledge that whatever I say
in the classroom there is a body of works out there that has
precedence over me. In other words, much as I would like to
tell my students certain things, there are, nevertheless, the
plays of Shakespeare, the poetry of Homer and of Dante. That
is to say, I don't live in my world alone. But I think one of the
dangers, as one grows older and is more driven by a certain
kind of habit, is that one begins to focus much more on oneself than on those voices outside—those works, those voices,
that, in the past, might have made one feel humble. I was very
interested, for example, to learn that Beethoven didn't like
very much to hear Mozart's works because he was afraid it
would abridge his own originality. And I have a philosopher
friend who told me once—he was in a certain moment of pro-
ductivity in his life—that he prefers not to read; he wants to
write; and reading—in other words, still learning—is somehow
in conflict with the act of producing.

DB: I believe very much in cycles. I believe in the cyclical presentation of works. I believe that a pianist who plays the cycle
of all the Beethoven sonatas obviously has a much broader
view of each individual sonata. I believe in the fluidity of life. I

believe in the fluidity of thought. We go through periods where we need to feed ourselves through the creations of others. And then, there are other periods where one has the need to isolate oneself from that. The way to progress is this paradoxical fluctuation.

EWS: I pick up a book by, let's say, an essayist. What I find that inspires me, or moves me, animates me, gets me excited, intellectually—if I'm in the mood to receive—is not simply a matter of information, it's a kind of spirit that you feel through the words: a sense of discovery; a sense of making one's way through material that suddenly impresses you as original or important and significant. I remember when I was about twenty-two or twenty-three, I read *The New Science* by Giambattista Vico, for the first time. It was so unusual a work that even the oddly antiquated and desperately striving style of the man has had a very lasting effect on my thought. Although it's a very eccentric book and is written by an obscure eighteenth-century Neapolitan philosopher and rhetorician, there was something about his fantastically original attitude toward history and the world that has remained with me. What he's talking about is always about how a human being makes his own history and can only understand it because he made it. That's my idea about secularity: that you don't rely on some outside miracle, outside force like the divinity, but that man makes his own history, Vico says, again and again. So, this is a very important insight and it informs me. I wonder, for a musician, whether there is that sense of insight and discovery in the work of other performers, other interpreters.

DB: Oh yes, no question about that. One must have the ability to hear, not only to listen.

EWS: What's the difference?

DB: You can listen without really hearing. I think it's wonderful that, in the English language, you have a difference in the two words. It's not in every language, is it? You must have the ability to hear what it is in the *rubato* of Cortot, or the sound of Rubinstein, or the phrasing of Arrau, whatever it may be. But at the same time, and almost parallel with it, you must find how to make it your own and how to apply it in your own way.

EWS: How does it happen, exactly? Tell me in your case, because one would think that, at one level, we're talking about a certain kind of imitation. For example, Arrau phrases a Chopin polonaise in a particular way; so being influenced by that, you reproduce the same phrase.

DB: Not necessarily. For instance, let's go back to the example of Furtwängler, because that's actually a very clear example. Furtwängler believed implicitly in the fact that it was not only permissible but necessary to have certain fluctuations of tempo, not only to achieve the expression of each individual molecule but, on the other hand, paradoxically, to achieve the sense of form, in order to have the ebb and flow. You needed to have these imperceptible fluctuations in order to achieve the sense of formal structure. Obviously, they have to be imperceptible. That means that one of the main principles of making music is the art of transition. I am very much aware of that when I listen to a Furtwängler performance. It does not mean that I will, necessarily, copy the outward manifestation of how he takes time in a certain phrase or how he makes a specific transition. I learn from him the function of that transition and

74

then try to find my own way of doing it. And very often, I have consciously tried to follow the example until I found my own way of doing it. And then, sometimes, the difference is not in the timing but in the volume, or in the intensity, in the transparency of the texture. And we are back to the point of time and space, which is the alphabet of music-making.

EWS: Language and music are really, in the end, temporal. They take place in time. Where does the element of space come in? Are you using it as a metaphor, or do you actually see it as a real thing?

DB: I see it as both: as a real thing and as a metaphor. If you take a work such as the slow movement of the Beethoven Ninth Symphony, and it is played with very little sense of the tension that is being created by the harmonies, you will need, obviously, a faster tempo than if you have all the inner tensions of the harmonies inside the chords pulling, pushing, and rubbing against each other. In that case, you will need more space, and you will need more time.

EWS: But how do you imagine the space? Is it a space that's from top to bottom and in depth, as well? In other words, is it that you are bringing the notes closer to each other to have a kind of tension, which they otherwise might not have?

DB: Yes. It's also somewhat the equivalent of perspective in painting: although the painting is on one plane, still you have the feeling that certain elements of the painting are nearer to you and others are farther away. Tonally, you can do that. At the extreme was the art of Horowitz playing the piano: you had the feeling that certain notes in the chord were literally in front of your face and others were miles away. It's a question of spacing, and it's a question of the vertical pressure on the horizontal. It can be done; and also with the piano, which is the instrument of illusion, really: everything you do on the piano is illusion. You create the illusion of a *crescendo*. You create the illusion of *diminuendo* on one note. You play through harmonic knowledge.

EWS: Do you want to listen to other pianists? Could that interfere with your hearing and playing?

DB: If I'm learning a new work, I don't want to hear another pianist until I have actually mastered the piece myself; but after that, I might get quite a lot out of hearing another pianist.

EWS: A lot of people say if you're writing a memoir, then you should read some of the other memoir writers. I found that it was better for me to master, through memory, my own story. It becomes very absorbing. You can't think of anything else. There, too, one feels a sense of space—that there are certain episodes to which you want to give a larger scope. But there, I feel it's metaphorical, in a way, because you're creating images in the minds of your reader. After all, they're just words on a page, and the transition from words on a page to figures—I think I prefer the word "figures," and shapes—is determined by the pacing, what you say, how you say it, the punctuation, the structure of the paragraph, and so on. That's very difficult to achieve if you're not completely focused on it yourself. But as I say, there are those voices in other things that constantly bombard one. And then, there's a question of who is the audience. To what extent do you, as a performer, pay attention to the audience, in the sense that you're trying to address them?

DB: Not so much. The day you decide to become a conductor, you have to do away with the natural instinct to want to be liked. The minute you have something individual to say, by definition, it will strike consonance in some and dissonance in others. I think that only mediocrity gets an uncontroversial re-action. And controversial has become almost a swear word in today's world, you know, "He's controversial."

EWS: They always say that about me.

DB: Well, I would take it as a great compliment.

EWS: Oh, I do, I do. But it's not meant that way. It's meant that this is a person who troubles the status quo in some way, which we want to preserve at all costs. But on the other hand, one also wants an audience. One doesn't want to be so repel-lent. The only time I ever saw Klemperer conduct, he was quite old and frail. He was conducting Bach's B minor Mass in London, and I remember the way he walked on stage, the way he sat at the podium. There was something profoundly unat-tractive about it, but compelling at the same time. But one has also seen conductors who are very flamboyant and there's a certain audience-pleasing quality to it. Do you think that's conscious?

DB: Oh, I think in some, it is, and in others, it isn't. There are some people who are naturally elegant —and this is wonder-ful—but I think that there are others who consciously try to become elegant.

EWS: And you can see that immediately. It doesn't work very well.

DB: It really doesn't work very well. But I think that one of the reasons why artistic creation is so important today is that it is a total opposite of being politically correct, of being uncontroversial.

EWS: Certainly, I feel it: that there's no point in writing material that makes people just feel good. And I've always been very interested not so much in making people comfortable but in making them uncomfortable. There are certain questions to be raised; there are certain attitudes to be addressed; in the end, there are certain clichés that you want to dismantle.

New York,
October 10, 1998

Chapter Four

※

EWS: We ought to begin with the fact that Wagner is a composer who, unlike almost any other composer, lends himself to conferences and discussions. And, of course, associated with the name of Wagner are a series of adjectives and nouns—there's Wagnerism, there's Wagnerian, there's a Wagnerite—and I just wanted to ask you, what is it that causes this extraordinary interest and devotion to Wagner? You wouldn't think of a Mozartian conference, and you wouldn't say that somebody is a Mozartian in the way that one is a Wagnerian.

DB: I think that the reasons are manifold. They stem from his musical personality; they stem from his personality outside music; they stem from the fact that he not only wrote music and the librettos to his own operas, but tried to revolutionize opera and to create the well-known concept of *Gesamtkunstwerk*. We can't really talk about Beethoven and the consequences; we can only speak about Debussy and the consequences in a very limited sense. But when we discuss Wagner and his consequences, we have to ask, did he have any influence—and if so, what kind of influence—on the way people viewed the music that preceded him? Did he have any effect on the history of the development of interpretation of the great classics, Mozart, Beethoven, etc.? And what influence, if any, did he have on the music that came after him? On the purely musical side of the twentieth century?

I think that if you examine these questions carefully, and you examine his writing about music (especially his book on conducting, which I have found not only interesting, but very useful), you will find a number of influences on music and performance. First of all, Wagner had a great understanding of, or intuition for (or perhaps a combination of the two), acoustics. He was the first person to have that, I think, except perhaps Berlioz, and in a certain way Liszt, although Liszt was more limited to the piano. By acoustics I mean the presence of sound in a room, the concept of time and space. Wagner really developed that concept musically. Which means that a lot of his criticism of performances of his own time, conducted by Mendelssohn and other people, was directed at what he considered a very superficial kind of interpretation of music, namely, one that took no risks, that didn't go to the abyss, that tried to find a golden path without having the extremes. Of course, this kind of performance leads to superficiality. This also affected the speed at which the music was performed, because if the content was poor, the speed had to be greater. Therefore Wagner complains bitterly about Mendelssohn's tempi.

How did he propose to fight that superficiality? In two ways. One, by developing the idea of a certain necessary flexibility of tempo, of certain imperceptible changes within the classical movements. (I'm talking now about his ideas about Beethoven, not about his own music—I'll come to that later if I may.) In other words, every sequence—every paragraph if you want to speak in literary terms—had its own *melos* and therefore required an imperceptible change of speed in order to be able to express the inherent content of that paragraph. All of these, of course, are concepts that are still being debated today. That these changes have to be imperceptible is evident, otherwise the form would break. But what Wagner really maintains is that unless you have the ability to guide the music in this way, you are not able to express all that is in it, and therefore you remain on the surface. He was diametrically opposed to a metronomic way of interpreting music. He had this idea of *Zeit und Raum,* time and space. Obviously tempo is not an independent factor: in order to sustain a slower tempo, which Wagner considered necessary for certain movements (not everything had to be slow, only certain movements and certain passages), he considered it an absolute necessity to slow down imperceptibly the second subject in a classical symphony where the first subject was dramatic—masculine, or whatever you want to call it—and the second was a contrast to that. But in order to make the slightly slower speed not only workable, but to allow it to express the content of the paragraph and to keep it within the context of the movement, there has to be, of course, some tonal compensation, and this is how he came to the concept of the continuity of sound: that sound tends to go to silence, unless it is sustained. From this came the whole concept not only of the color of sound—which is what so many people talk about today and which has led to (to my mind) superficial ideas about the "international sound of orchestras"—but of the weight of sound. And Wagner was more interested in the weight of the sound.

Of course, it was easier for him to deal with that concept then, because the minute you talk about weight you also talk about harmony. And since this was all pre-atonal music, the harmonic fundamental was much stronger than it is now. And therefore, tied to the gravity of the harmony, he was able to create more and more tension through the continuity of sound, and this imperceptible slowing down of the tempo went practically unnoticed. Then somehow at the end, in an unnoticeable way, you came back. These two words, "imperceptible" and "unnoticeable," are very important because this is the art of transition. What I'm trying to say by this is that, through these two concepts, Wagner influenced the way the whole world, without exception, looked at the music that had come before him, the classics, mostly German or middle or central European music—Mozart, Beethoven, Schubert, Schumann, etc.—without mentioning that of his contemporaries.

Therefore, until the Second World War, you couldn't ignore Wagner's ideas, whether you knew that they came from Wagner or not. They just became tradition. And whether the conductors were Furtwängler, Weingartner, Bruno Walter, or even, in a way, Toscanini, who obviously went absolutely against all these ideas, they could not refrain from occupying themselves with these principles. The same goes for the instrumentalists, not only for orchestras, but for people like Hans von Bülow and D'Albert. And this we know neither from hearsay, nor even from the relative perfection or precision of recordings, but from the editions they made of the Beethoven sonatas, for instance. I've studied them very carefully, both the Bülow edition and the D'Albert edition, and you see all these principles of the slight modification of tempo, on through Schnabel, Edwin Fischer, Backhaus, etc. All this would have been unthinkable without Wagner's ideas. So, in this way, he influenced a whole history of interpretation of music, to the point that the reaction that came in this century—the sort of new objectivity, *die neue Sachlichkeit* it was called in Germany, was an attempt to fight this. What we are experiencing now, in the last whatever number of years, with the revival of historical practices and playing on period instruments, is also, in fact—whether knowingly or not—a reaction against this Wagnerian concept of the continuity of sound. The principle of these instruments and this way of making music is precisely to articulate more and to be able to cut the sound and to cut the harmonic pressure of the music.

When he came to write his own music, he developed all these principles to the extreme. In fact, Wagner, to my mind, developed each expressive element, in sound production and music expression, and to its extreme—like an elastic that is stretched to its extreme. He created a form in the operas that did away with the separation of musical numbers, arias, etc. In other words, he constantly worked with continuity. He developed harmony in a very, very personal way, and in many directions. One always talks in general about Wagnerian harmonies, but *Tristan und Isolde* is one world, *Die Meistersinger* is a completely different world, and to my mind *Parsifal* is yet another world.

The development of the interpretation of his own music— and this is pure intuition and feeling, I have no proof of this —I find is tied much more to the spirit of the time, to the Zeitgeist and to the nonmusical ideas that preoccupied people. And you find, in a lot of the performances from the 1920s until after the Second World War, something which I find has much in common with Nazi monumentality, which is also evident in architecture and in the other arts. There is something bombastic, loud, uncouth, not very refined or subtle, in the colors and in the balance.

In fact, the first conscious preoccupation, I think, with balance and with the strict adherence to the dynamics of the works came from people like Rudolf Kempe, who was to my mind a very underrated German conductor who had a great feeling for sound and for balance, and then, of course, Pierre Boulez in his by now famous production of the *Ring* tetralogy with the great French theater director Patrice Chéreau in 1976 at Bayreuth. I think that this is what demystified the musical aspect—I'm not talking now about the world of ideas. And, as in all other music, I find Furtwängler's interpretation of Wagner not only in a class of its own—this is a matter of taste—but on a path of its own, where even in the most obvious, open moments, like in the *Meistersinger* overture, there is an uncanny and unlimited strength in the search for understanding. I think Furtwängler was an artist who had a great understanding of the tragic element of music—I mean tragic in the mythological sense, i.e., you must journey to hell before you can achieve catharsis, the climax, or whatever you are looking for. There was in Furtwängler's work an ever-present search for the ground or the underground, a sort of archeological expedition, to understand where each development came from, what was before this openness of the C major chords that appear so often in *Die Meistersinger*, how did they happen to have this particular significance. Therefore, he was a master of the flow and ebb of the music. Furtwängler is one of the few conductors who had the courage not only to slow down for expressive reasons, but to push on when necessary.

EWS: Do you think there is a tendency in Wagner's work—let's say in *Tristan* and even, to a degree, in *Parsifal*—to move toward not just the notion of flow and transition and becoming, but also a kind of indeterminacy which, in a certain sense, prepares one for atonality?

DB: I don't think so. I think that Wagner knew exactly what he wanted, and the effect of what he wrote would produce, and I don't mean effect in the superficial, banal way, but in the deepest sense. Maybe part of his mistake is that he tried, in a slightly over-Teutonic way, to systemize something that has to do more with the realm of feeling in music: that absolutely necessary relationship between manipulation and yielding, which to me is the basis of all music-making, in fact, of human existence. So when he leads us into a blurred, indefinite area, I think then he is manipulating. I think he knows perfectly well what he is doing . . .

EWS: Or is there a particular aim that he has in mind?

DB: Yes, I mean manipulating in a positive sense. He is leading us out because he knows that he will always bring us back. There is a wonderful sentence, which I unfortunately cannot quote precisely, from Schoenberg's book on harmony, about not ever leading the ear into foreign lands, harmonically speaking. And I think that when Wagner does that, either in the tempo in the dynamic or in the harmonies, it is with a very conscious idea behind it. He wants to give us the feeling that we are lost, in order to then bring us back with great certainty. He uses very clearly defined technical means to do this. You see it very often in the way he divides the strings. In *Rheingold* especially, there is a division of half of the section: it says *die Hälfte,* "half," then it says, "the first half," and then it says "the second half." I interpret that half as meaning left and right: the first half means the first four stands if you're playing with eight stands, and the second half means the second, the last four stands. And, of course, in these nebulous areas, he very often approaches the sound coming from the back of the sections, and a feeling of uncertainty is further developed by *tremolo* turns into measured sixteenths in the strings; that immediately gives you a feeling of rhythm. If you examine that

carefully, you see that you can add to the feeling of indefinite-
ness that he creates by being free with the tempo during the
tremolo, but obviously, if you are going to give its full meaning,
you have to adopt a very strict tempo when the measured
movement of the sixteenths in the strings begins.

EWS: But that raises a question about the strictly musical and
interpretive aspect of putting Wagner on the stage and bringing him to life. You're a conductor who lives in Wagner, in a
sense; you play him, you think about him; where do you feel
the limits of your freedom are with Wagner? In other words,
do you feel that you can, as Toscanini did, double parts that
are not written that way, or add and subtract from what is
given? Or do you feel that you are guided by a literal approach
to the text, where perhaps the thing is the balance between
what you think of as the spirit of the work versus the literal
manifestation of the work on a piece of paper, which is the
score, after all. The third element, of course, is tradition. Tradition could just be the last bad performance that was done,
but it also means that you've obviously benefited from what
you've listened to, and you are in a line with a number of conductors, which is an element, too, in the interpretation.

DB: I think that when one speaks about the literal understanding of a work of music, one has to be very specific about
it, because nowadays when one talks about music performance, one talks mostly about tempo. Is he free? In other
words, does he take liberties with the tempo or does he play
like a metronome? I'm oversimplifying it, obviously, for the
sake of the clarity of the argument. But I think that, in a way,
so many concepts have become superficial through overuse.
They are blurred. *Literal* to me means that you do what is written, but you do *all* of what is written, not only the part that is

easy to judge. In other words, if there is a phrase that is very difficult, almost impossible, to play *legato*, that has no break in it, that is seamless and has a tremendous intensity, and you do not play it that way, that for me is not literal. In other words, literal has to be adjusted from the line of least resistance to the line of most resistance. In music-making, the only line that is valuable is the line of most resistance. Therefore, when you talk about literalness, you have to talk about changing text or-chestration; you have to talk about tempo; you have to talk about dynamics; you have to talk about balance; and you have to talk about the length of the notes. The only work of Wagner where I think one would be slightly justified in wanting to change the orchestration, even on a very small scale, is *The Ring*, for the simple reason that *The Ring*, although it was first performed in complete form in Bayreuth, was not written for the house in Bayreuth. The only work of Wagner that was writ-ten for that house was *Parsifal*. And Wagner himself, who was present at all the rehearsals of *Parsifal*, wanted to reorches-trate certain passages of *The Ring* after his experiences in that house.

EWS: For Bayreuth?

DB: Yes. I think other than that, Wagner's mastery of instru-mentation—and of the varying levels of volume and density of sound that are created by the different instruments of the or-chestra—is so masterly that there is no need to even think about changing it. There is always something that has to be done to the sound so that it does produce the necessary effect as it is written.

EWS: That's true principally of the works performed in Bay-reuth. If you were to perform, let's say, *The Ring* in Bayreuth,

as you have, or *Tristan,* or *Parsifal,* then a different set of practices obtains that . . .

DB: I have conducted *Tristan* for many, many years in Bayreuth. I have also conducted *Tristan* with an open pit. I have
conducted the second act of *Tristan,* often in concert form.
I've conducted *Parsifal* and *Walküre* and *Siegfried,* also in an
open pit at the State Opera in Berlin. So, I have had the opportunity to compare the two. I think the main difference, of
course, is the balance between orchestra and stage: in Bayreuth, you can really play the loud passages full out, which you
cannot do in an open pit.

EWS: Can you describe what it's like to play in Bayreuth as
opposed to somewhere else?

DB: As you know, the pit in Bayreuth is mostly covered, and it
goes down in steps, so that you do not get, as you do in an
open pit, the sound directly from the pit to the audience. And
therefore, you, as a listener, do not have to mix it with the
sound that you get from the singers on the stage. You get it already mixed, and this is why it is often so mellow, so round,
and so creamy. The pit itself, acoustically speaking, is very res-
onant; it has a tendency to be too loud, and there, the reaction
when you first start playing there is to try and play too softly,
because you think it's too loud, and it takes some time to get
used to it. I would compare the pit at Bayreuth to deep-sea div-
ing. When you are underwater and you have a problem with
your equipment, you can really use only your brain and some
movements to get out of the difficulty and to climb to the
surface. You don't get anywhere with aggression, with elbow-
pushing, because the water is much too strong. And, in a way,

the Bayreuth pit is like this, too. The moment there is slight difficulty with the precision, there is no point in trying to beat angularly in the hope that everybody will count to that, because it doesn't happen. It's a question of giving an idea of when the next important moment is coming, and then everybody assembles. In other words, it is a question of not going to the musician or the section in question and beating angularly in his eyes, but rather of bringing him to you. And all kinds of round movements can help you do that.

EWS: So, to incorporate the sound rather than let it . . .

DB: Yes. And in fact, the conductors that have had difficulties acoustically in the pit at Bayreuth have been conductors who have a very angular way of conducting. But, as you mentioned as we were walking here, Wagner had a preoccupation with everything that was round, and I think this is part of his whole personality: he hated anything that was angular or clearly defined.

EWS: If I could just mention that I was very surprised this summer: you associate a performance at a place like Bayreuth with great formality, and the audience is mostly dressed in tails and tuxedos, and evening dresses, and so on. The temperature was about 150 degrees the day I went—it was extremely hot, and the pit, where the orchestra is, under the stage, so to speak, is not known for its coolness. Elena Barenboim and I went backstage after the first act, and there was Daniel in a T-shirt and shorts, and the orchestra in the most informal clothes you can imagine. It's a very strange kind of dissonance to see that.

DB: It takes a little getting used to.

EWS: Of course, all the actors and the singers in their costumes, you wonder how they can make it through the thing, because it is incredibly hot.

DB: Well, not in this production, but in the former production of *Tristan* that I conducted, which was staged by Jean-Pierre Ponnelle, King Marke came on stage in a huge fur coat. And poor Matti Salminen, who is a giant anyway, I think he was . . .

EWS: . . . dying. Yes, and of course, all the operas are set in the north. They're not about happy southern folk like us. So, the characters tend to be very heavily dressed. But having said all the things you've said about conducting . . .

DB: There is one more thing about the difference between conducting in the pit at Bayreuth and in an open pit, for example at the State Opera pit in Berlin. The main difference is that at the State Opera you have to start all the *crescendos* a little later than you would in a covered pit because otherwise you get too loud too soon; and you must come down with the *diminuendos* obviously a little quicker, and you cannot sustain loud chords in the brass as long as you can in Bayreuth. At first, this might seem like a thinning out of the musical material, but it doesn't necessarily have to be like that because you get an orchestral presence; you get an active participation from the orchestra in an open pit that you cannot get in Bayreuth. In a work like *Parsifal,* it makes no difference. On the contrary, I think that anybody who conducts *Parsifal* but has not conducted it in Bayreuth has not really conducted *Parsifal*. It was written for that acoustic, for that place, and it needs to be done there. But even in *The Ring*—I did, for instance, the new production of *Siegfried* in Berlin last year—I think that you have to be very open and see that there are advantages and disadvantages in both.

EWS: But Bayreuth is obviously a place you like to conduct in.

DB: Oh, for these works, it is absolutely a necessity. It is another level.

EWS: Now to move from Bayreuth, the place, to Bayreuth, the idea, or the ideology. There is a lot of baggage involved in Wagner's operas. There is, as you said earlier, all the prose-writing. And there is also the extremely problematic material of the dramas themselves. Obviously, sexuality is quite pronounced—and unprecedented before Wagner—in those works. Similarly, violence of one sort or another.

DB: Well, Verdi is not exactly mild.

EWS: No, no, of course.

DB: I saw *Otello* a few nights ago.

EWS: But it's the combination that is special to Wagner, plus, of course, all of Wagner's writing from the beginning to the very end of his career, when he was concerned about a lot of the ideology having to do with German culture and the Jews, and so forth, in the period of *Parsifal*. You are dealing with a composer who is unique in that way, and this is obviously one of the aspects of Wagner that is problematic. And the other is what has been discussed at many of the talks at this conference—the association of Wagner and Bayreuth with the Nazi period and the use made of Wagner during the Nazi period.

The thing that you can obviously inform us about and illuminate is: What is it like as a conductor to face all of these issues in the productions that you deal with? To what extent is there a kind of interplay or even an antagonism? In many respects, Wagner's work is really all about antitheses, contradictions.

DB: Within himself, too.

EWS: Within himself, absolutely. I think it would be somehow basically wrong from an interpretive point of view to mute them, and to say, oh, they're really not there; there's this quite serene, marvelous world that he's produced of heroes and gods and goddesses. That's nonsense. But the question is, given your background: What is it like to confront this—whether as somebody preparing a production, or conducting it, or, as we are now, thinking about it?

DB: Well, I hope you have time because I can't answer this briefly. A few things have to be made clear. First of all, there is Wagner the composer. Then, there's Wagner the writer of his own librettos—in other words, everything that is tied to the music. Then, there is Wagner the writer on artistic matters. And then, there is Wagner the political writer—in this case, primarily the anti-Semitic political writer. These are four different aspects to his work.

But before discussing them, I think it is worth examining the history of production in Bayreuth. Bayreuth began, under Wagner, as a great experimental theater. The whole world attended the world premiere of *The Ring* in 1876. Wagner also had, for his time, absolutely the most revolutionary and progressive ideas. He was a man of such forceful talent that he also invented the notion of the covered pit, such as it was constructed in Bayreuth. The pit at Bayreuth has been accepted by all modern acousticians as absolutely perfect; not only that, it is impossible to imitate. Which shows you that his talents and his genius went far beyond composing music.

He started the theater in Bayreuth in 1876, but shortly afterward, he had to close the theater because he didn't have any money. The year of the world premiere of *Parsifal* was 1882. He died in 1883. As is often the case with great artists, they inspire either unrestrained adulation or uncontrolled hatred, and Wagner is a prime example of this. His widow, Cosima, and everybody who worked with him then, worked in an atmosphere of uncritical adulation and fought to preserve every little snippet of an idea that the master might have had, which is the most un-Wagnerian thing you can do, because he was exactly the opposite himself. He was a revolutionary; he rethought and redid and undid everything in order to create it anew. Therefore, this whole fight to retain the theater at Bayreuth as it had been under Wagner, to my mind made Bayreuth devoid of one of the most important characteristics of Wagner the artist. Productions there stayed almost exactly the same, in fact, until the Second World War. *The Ring,* for example, remained the same production except for adaptations to technological developments such as electricity, etc., from 1876 until at least the 1920s—that's nearly fifty years. Bayreuth was the most conservative, unthoughtful theater in the whole world. This was also caused, in the twenties, by the rise of German nationalism and the type of conductors who would agree to conduct at Bayreuth: Bruno Walter never conducted there; Klemperer didn't conduct there; Fritz Busch, who was not a Jew but felt morally very strongly about the way the Jews were being treated, would not conduct there. I'm talking about the *beginning* of the Nazi era if not before. Busch then left Germany in protest with the rest of his family, conducted once, and never came again, because he found the whole atmosphere intolerable. Even Hans Mayer, the great Wagner theorist who was there as a young man, recalls it as being absolutely intolerable.

So, that conservatism stuck in the interpretation of the works. In other words, it was not in the *nature* of the works but in their *interpretation* at Bayreuth. In fact, it went, as I've said before, against the innate character of the works. Emil Pretorius was there in the thirties; and with Furtwängler, there was some kind of new idea, but basically, it remained the same. I think it is important to acknowledge that Bayreuth, from 1876 until the Second World War, was the most conservative, narrow-minded theater in the whole world.

When the festival was reopened in 1951 by Wagner's two grandsons, Wieland and Wolfgang, the whole idea of the new Bayreuth was developed. Wieland's idea was that the music is written out and clearly defined, but the staging is not written out and, therefore, has to be adapted to the aesthetic necessities of the times. And this is, of course, at the root of stage production and opera production. What really is expected? I mean, we have a written score in front of us, but what is literal in terms of staging? Wieland tried to make Bayreuth the most progressive place, in those terms, and he did. And in fact, since 1951, Bayreuth has become exactly the opposite of what it was before: a place where everything is rethought, a place where all the productions are made to coincide with the ideas of the people who stage them—Wieland, and then Wolfgang, and then people like Patrice Chéreau, Götz Friedrich, Harry Kupfer, and now Heiner Müller.

I came to Wagner relatively late—for me in any case. The musical education that I got and the ambience that I lived in revolved much more around piano, instrumental, symphonic, and chamber music. I went to hear song recitals; I went to hear string quartets; and I went to hear symphony orchestras; I rarely went to the opera. When I was nine, my family and I moved to Israel. The Israel Opera was rather poor in those days, but Wagner wasn't played in any case, so I had no real contact, I mean active contact, until I was nearly twenty years old.

EWS: What was the first Wagner you saw, do you remember?

DB: I think *Tristan*. So, I came to Wagner first of all from a purely musical and orchestral point of view. And I became fascinated with the way every element can really be examined individually, and with the whole idea of orchestration and of the weight and continuity of sound. And I became very interested in Wagner through his writings about music, and conducting, etc. So, this was the main thing that interested me first, and I did not occupy myself with the world of ideas at that stage. I must say, in those days, I had no idea I would end up conducting operas. I was not even conducting the English Chamber Orchestra, let alone in Bayreuth, so nothing was further from my mind. And I approached Wagner from the works that were closer to me, and that had an influence on Wagner as a musician: Beethoven first of all; then, of course, Berlioz and Liszt; and in a way, Bruckner, although he was not an influence on Wagner, but I was from early on attached to the music of Bruckner. The study of Wagner—Wagner's music—was of great help to me, not only in eventually performing his own works, but in understanding many, many other styles of music. And that goes as far as Debussy—post-Wagner, too. I will never forget how it struck me the first time I conducted Debussy's *La Mer,* and I suddenly found the same combinations of instruments in unison—trumpet and English horn, or trumpet and oboe, as in the prelude to *Parsifal*—that only Wagner had used before him. In other words, the coloristic element of Wagner is also very important. In any case, this is what really fascinated me in his work and in his writings about music. And his writing on the Beethoven symphonies and on conducting in general had a great influence on my whole way of looking at his music and of playing it. And then, as I became more and more connected with the pieces, I started preparing to conduct the operas, and this was the first time that I occupied myself with Wagner's writing on the subjects other than the music itself—i.e., the texts that Wagner wrote for his own operas and his ideological writings.

EWS: What did you think about his views on the Jews and music, for example, that really are quite central to a lot of what he wrote? And subsequently, what did you think about the modern musicological and cultural interpretations of Wagner that stress or try to stress the extent to which some of those ideas he discusses in the prose works are carried over into the operas? Interestingly, anti-Semitism and Wagner was not really a big topic until fairly recently, although Adorno pioneered it in his early book on Wagner, but one of the things that he says there is, of course, that Mime and Beckmesser, to name two characters, are, in fact, caricatures of Jews, and that if you pay close attention to that strand in the work—I mean in the prose work—you can find it in the operas. Given the history of association between Wagner and National Socialism—and the horrendous results of that association in the Holocaust—there is a massive weight there that one has to deal with somehow, in looking at the work. You're a Jew, and I don't need to add that I'm a Palestinian, so it's an interesting . . .

DB: We are both Semitic. So, he was against both of us!

EWS: We'll come to Wagner and the Palestinians later. But now, we're talking about Wagner and the Jews. It's a question that, in a certain sense, can't be avoided. If I might just add one other thing to it and that is that, in his operas, Wagner uses Jewish caricatures to represent characters who themselves are not Jewish. I mean, Mime is not Jewish in the work—he's not identified that way—and the same is true about Beckmesser. Whereas in his prose works, Wagner does speak directly about Jews.

DB: Well, I think it's obvious that Wagner's anti-Semitic views and writings are monstrous. There is no way around that. And I must say that if I, in a naïvely sentimental way, try to think which of the great composers of the past I would love to spend twenty-four hours with if I could, Wagner doesn't come to mind. I'd love to follow Mozart around for twenty-four hours; I'm sure it would be very entertaining, amusing, edifying, but Wagner, no.

EWS: You wouldn't invite him to dinner.

DB: Wagner? I might invite him to dinner for study purposes, but not for enjoyment.

EWS: Put a glass wall between you.

DB: But in other words, the person, Wagner, is absolutely appalling, despicable, and, in a way, very difficult to put together with the music he wrote, which so often has exactly the opposite kind of feelings. It is noble, generous, etc. But now we are entering into the whole discussion of whether it is moral or not, etc., and this becomes too involved in a discussion. But suffice it to say for now that Wagner's anti-Semitism was monstrous. That he used a lot of, at the time, common terminology for what could be described as salon anti-Semitism, and that he had all sorts of rationalizations about it, does not make it any less monstrous. He also used some abominable phrases which can be, at best, interpreted as being said in the heat of the moment—that Jews should be burned, etc. Whether or not he meant these things figuratively can be discussed. The fact remains that he was a horrific anti-Semite. I do know the Nazis used, misused, and abused Wagner's ideas or thoughts —I think this has to be said—beyond what he might have had in mind. Anti-Semitism was not invented by Adolf Hitler, and it was certainly not invented by Richard Wagner. It existed for generations and generations and centuries before. The difference between National Socialism and the earlier forms of anti-Semitism is that the Nazis were the first, to my knowledge, to evolve a systematic plan to exterminate the Jews. And I don't think Wagner can be made responsible for that, even though a lot of the Nazi thinkers, if you want to call them that, often quote Wagner as their precursor. It also needs to be said, for clarity's sake, that, in the operas themselves, there is not one Jewish character. There is not one anti-Semitic remark. There is nothing in any one of the ten great operas of Wagner even remotely approaching a character like Shylock. That you can interpret Mime or Beckmesser in a certain anti-Semitic way (in the same way, you can also interpret *The Flying Dutchman* as the errant Jew), this is a question that speaks not about Wagner, but about our imagination and how our imagination is developed, coming into contact with those works.

EWS: Yes, but it's more than that, Daniel, if I might interject something. You can say that it's our imagination, but it's also known, I think, that Wagner drew on things available to him in his culture: images, which came from the standard language; ideas, and images, of anti-Semitic thought.

DB: Judaism was a subject of parody, there is no question about that. It was a subject of parody, and I'm sure that in the privacy of Wagner's house Wahnfried, he and Cosima very often imitated Mime with a Jewish accent and with Jewish mannerisms, etc.; I don't deny that for one moment. On the other hand, you have to say that Wagner was, in that respect, artistically very open and, I would say, courageous, too. If he'd really wanted to make the operas an artistic expression of his anti-Semitism, he would have called a spade a spade, and he didn't. In other words, that he ridiculed the Jews is absolutely clear, but I don't think that this is an inherent part of the works.

EWS: But what about the other side of it; I mean, Wagner's operas are full of associations—not mental associations, but groups of people—with which he seems to have been fascinated just as he was fascinated with outsiders. That is to say, you have the Meistersinger Guild in *Meistersinger*; you have the Brotherhood of the Grail in *Parsifal*; you have the tribes in *The Ring*; and in situations like that, the group sense is part of the opera. Well, you have a moment in *Meistersinger* in the last act where Hans Sachs speaks out, in a way that he doesn't speak before, about holy German art and warns against the dangers to it from the outside. One could say that most of Wagner's work, *The Ring* and *Meistersinger* in particular, is full of a kind of both implicit and explicit German nationalism. His prose writings are full of this also. There was a particular mission, and he appointed himself its guardian, its renewer, its revolutionary, its transformer, and so on; he played a particular role. And I just wonder whether you feel that in something that is this explicit, the nationalism has to be taken literally.

DB: I think that it must be clear also that we cannot speak about German nationalism in the way that we can speak about French nationalism or Italian nationalism in art, because the Nazi image of the German nationalism is so strong. But there is something specifically German about some music in the same way that there is something specifically in French . . .

EWS: And you've spoken about a particular German orchestral sound.

DB: Right, and what I will say may be very shocking, because *Meistersinger* has been considered for so many years as a sort of Nazi ideological work because of all that. But I think, in fact, that it is a critique of the society as it is today. That's why I think *Meistersinger* is a very important work now, in this sort of global culture that makes Paris, Tokyo, and New York all the same. I think that this is one of the main subjects of *Meistersinger*. One of the subjects of *Meistersinger* is, of course, the relation between mediocrity and genius, between artist and dilettante, between the new and the old in the person of Stolzing.

EWS: And the relationship between discipline and inspiration.

DB: Discipline and inspiration. Stolzing is a highly talented newcomer without the experience—in other words, incomplete—and can be completed only with the experience that he learns through Sachs. So, it is a combination of talent and progressive thought, if you want, with the experience of tradition that makes the great artist. And this is what brings us in the end, the third act, after Beckmesser makes a fool of himself with his song, and Walther wins the prize, when Hans Sachs makes his final statement in praise of German art. It is this statement that has led to so much discussion, and to my mind, misuse, because what he is talking about precisely are the values of art in its fullest form, which he associates with German art. I don't think there's anything wrong with that; the fact that there is German art, a German style of playing, can be absolutely proven. There is a definite German string sound: a "German triplet" is a triplet where the first note of the triplet is drawn out to make a broad triplet; a "German upbeat" is a broad upbeat. Why? Because the language is like this. When you say *la lune,* the upbeat is short; when you say *der Mond,* it has to be longer and it has to be separated. This is the terminology, and this doesn't have to inspire any fear. What Sachs is saying in that speech is that, basically, there is a combination of text, of word and music, in the Prize Song, as performed by Stolzing, which leads to the most noble form of expression of German art. That is all. In other words, it is against what could be described as Nazi ideology, the masters without the talent, only the acceptance of what is already known. Beckmesser is a dangerous character. On top of being funny, he's dangerous because he thinks that by knowing all the rules better than anybody else, he is a greater artist; of course, he is not. Now, when you take this last monologue of Hans Sachs, and you take it out of the context of what has happened in the opera before and what it is meant to mean, and you put it into the political rally and Nuremberg, then its meaning becomes totally different, and this has led to it being interpreted as it is.

EWS: I don't know whether I'm completely convinced by that. In other words, I agree with you that it shouldn't be taken out of context, and I think you're absolutely right to say that the opera as a whole is about those relationships that we spoke about earlier—between innovation, tradition, genius, and discipline, and so on. What is striking about it is—forgetting about the context and the consequences at the Nuremberg rallies—that there is a transformation, first of all, from the domestic world, the cobblers, the streets of Nuremberg to this vast official gathering-place where the Meistersingers and the townsfolk all get together, and it is a rally of some sort. In addition, Sachs is proclaimed as the great figure for the city because he has understood these things, and the sound of the opera changes at the point that he begins to talk about this: a sort of menacing, chromatic, threatening sound comes out of the orchestra as he sings, and what he's talking about is *listen to your German masters.* In other words, there's a sense, in the opera, that what he's really saying is that once one acknowledges the presence of someone new and gifted like Stolzing, there is nevertheless the need to follow, and the collective is, in a sense, most important. Finally, there's the idea of the outside as threatening: there's a kind of xenophobic quality *in* the opera—which is troubling.

DB: But if you read German books from the 1920s, for instance, there is a remarkable book by Furtwängler's composition teacher. I think it was a biography of Beethoven, at the end of which there is a wonderful analysis of the first movement of the *Eroica,* but the book is unreadable because he is continually talking about German art, the German way of producing sound, the German way of phrasing, the German this and the German that, but this is really all pre-Nazi.

EWS: No, I agree. And it's not only German; you find it, for example, in French writing of the end of the nineteenth century, *la science française, la civilisation française*.

DB: Debussy had written on his visiting card: *Claude Debussy, musicien français*.

EWS: So, one has to take seriously these ideas of competing, and in my opinion, virulent nationalism. I don't think they can be subsumed entirely within the work.

DB: No, but I think Germans were convinced, and some of them still are convinced today, that they invented music among the many other things that they invented. And in a certain way, they did. I would like to speak about the whole problem of Wagner in Israel. In 1936, Toscanini, who had been in Bayreuth, as you know, in 1930 and I think 1931, refused to go back to Bayreuth because of the Nazis and I think because of Hitler's presence in Bayreuth. He went instead to Tel Aviv where the then Palestine Philharmonic Orchestra was founded by Bronislaw Huberman and conducted the first opening concerts of the orchestra. In the program, there was Brahms's Second Symphony, there were some Rossini overtures, and also the preludes to Act 1 and Act 3 of *Lohengrin*. Nobody had a word to say about it; nobody criticized him; the orchestra was very happy to play it. Wagner's anti-Semitism was as well known then as it is now, so therefore the whole problem of playing Wagner in Israel has nothing to do with his anti-Semitism. What actually happened after that was that, after Kristallnacht in November 1938, the orchestra, which is a collective group of musicians who govern themselves and run themselves to this day, decided that because of the association—the Nazis' use of Wagner's music and how it led to the burning of the books—they refused to play any more Wagner. This is all there is to it. Everything that has come since then has been the reaction of people from outside the orchestra, some in favor, some absolutely against. Why am I telling you this? Because I think this shows very clearly that one has to distinguish between Wagner's anti-Semitism, which is monstrous and despicable and worse than the sort of normal, shall we say, accepted-unacceptable level of anti-Semitism and the use the Nazis made of it. I have met people who absolutely cannot listen to Wagner. A lady who came to see me in Tel Aviv when the whole Wagner debate was taking place said, "How can you want to play that? I saw my family taken to the gas chambers to the sound of the *Meistersinger* overture. Why should I listen to that?" Simple answer: there is no reason why she should listen to it. I don't think that Wagner should be forced on anybody, and the fact that he has inspired such extreme feelings, both pro and con, since his death, doesn't mean to say that we don't have some civic obligations. Therefore, my suggestion at the time was that the orchestra, which was willing to play, should not play it in a subscription concert where anybody who has been a loyal subscriber to the Israel Philharmonic for so many years would be forced to listen to something that they didn't want to listen to. These musicians were the descendants of the musicians who had voted in 1938 to boycott, so, in effect, they were redoing the vote and closing the circle. But if somebody does not make these associations, especially since these associations do not stem from Wagner himself, he should be able to hear it. Therefore, my suggestion was that it should be played in a non-subscription concert of the Israel Philharmonic where anybody who didn't want to hear it didn't have to, and anybody who wanted to go had to go and buy a ticket for that specific concert. And the fact that this was not allowed to happen is a reflection of a kind of political abuse and of all sorts of ideas that again have nothing to do with Wagner's music. And this is really the chapter of Wagner and Judaism.

QUESTION (from the audience at Columbia University): I will begin, if I may, by asking Mr. Barenboim—you relayed in your autobiography that you were invited by Furtwängler to play for the Berlin Philharmonic, and that your father refused to let you do that when you were young, and obviously, you now have a career in Germany. Was there a moment for you, obviously with the passage of time, the change in the creation of a democratic government in Germany after the war, where you were able to make that step? Was it a clear moment or was it simply something that happened?

DB: Obviously, otherwise I wouldn't be there now. In other words, when Furtwängler invited me and my father refused, it was in 1954. The summer of 1954, I was still eleven years old, I cannot claim that I had fully developed ideas about this. I was told by my father what it meant, that the war had only been over for nine years, the atrocities, not only of the war, but of the Holocaust, the concentration camps, etc., etc., etc. And that's why my father felt that this invitation should not be accepted and I, naturally, agreed with that. I must also say in retrospect, as much as I would have loved nothing more, musically speaking, than to have played with Furtwängler, from the perspective of today I think he was absolutely right. I then became more and more acquainted with certain aspects also of Israeli thought in relation to Germany and Austria and a lot of details, which I found not really thought-out, like for instance the fact that there were diplomatic relations established between Israel and Austria very early on, and not with

Germany. I don't think Austria was any milder in its way of looking at Jewish extermination. And there were many other problems, plus the fact that we came into contact with so many other parts of the German past, including the trial of Adolph Eichmann in Jerusalem in 1961. And from that I made up my mind that I wanted to go and play in Germany and try and see how I felt. I must say that by then I had the total support of both my parents to do that. I was twenty when I first went to Germany, so I was, in a way, grown up, and I had been traveling alone in the world for a long time, but this subject being of such importance, I obviously talked to my parents about it and had their full support, and that's how I started going to Germany.

QUESTION: I was in Bayreuth in 1991, and I saw the production of *Das Rheingold* that Maestro Barenboim had done, and I've always been a great admirer of Mr. Barenboim's musicianship. However, this production of *Das Rheingold*, which was directed by Harry Kupfer, had the most appalling anti-Semitism in it that I've ever encountered. In the production, the Alberich character is a blatant copy of the kinds of caricature of Jews that were put in *Der Stürmer*, the Nazi newspaper, and to see this man gallivanting on stage as such a caricature of a Jew, and then, near the end of the opera, when he's captured by Wotan and Loge—they not only capture him, but take a metal pole and stick it between his legs and twist it and he's tortured on stage, ends up completely bloody—to see this in Bayreuth, where there already has been this experience with Nazis and this kind of torture, I couldn't understand how a Jewish conductor could take part in such a production.

DB: I can only tell you that if the violence of the action offended you, I'm sorry, and you have every right to have this kind of sentiment. The rest is your pure interpretation and imagination. I can assure you, I worked very carefully with Harry Kupfer on the production of this. We spoke openly about every subject that was treated in this staging. Never was there an intention, never was there an idea on Kupfer's side to make a Jewish character out of Alberich, or anybody else. Therefore, I'm afraid I have to tell you this: it really says more about how you saw it rather than what it really was.

QUESTION: You have omitted saying anything about the Wagner family embracing Hitler in Bayreuth in the 1930s.

DB: I haven't omitted it, it's just not a subject that was discussed. During the 1930s, it is known that Winifred Wagner was a great sympathizer of Hitler and that he visited her house and used Bayreuth as his base. The Wagner family, I suppose, not unlike many other families, have people who think in different ways. One of Winifred's daughters, Friedlinde, escaped, was asked to come back by her mother, and then Hitler's agents were sent to Switzerland to ask her to return. She refused; then, with Toscanini's help, she made her way to Argentina and ended up in New York in the forties, became an American citizen, and always was a fervent anti-Nazi. Other members had opposing views, and I think that the criticism that has been leveled at the Wagner family has to be limited to the people who really had this idea. One cannot attribute a collective guilt to the whole family. In fact, one of Wagner's great-grandsons [Gottfried] gave a seminar at the Ben Gurion University in Beersheva. His sister visited Israel, and I don't think that you can accuse this generation of a kind of collective guilt.

QUESTION: Dealing with the issue of the collective anti-Semitism: as we all know reading Wagner's work, he was terribly opportunistic. At one point in his life, he was an anarchist; he was expelled from Dresden. When he sensed the German empire becoming ascendant after 1870, he became a monarchist. On the other hand, it seems to me that, in his anti-Semitism, the contradiction extends to his personal life.

DB: Oh, I think that anti-Semitism was probably uppermost in his thoughts and in his list of priorities until the moment that it affected his pocket or his own need for help, artistic or monetary. I then think he would even have become a Zionist, excuse me. I must tell you, for a long time—ever since I agreed to do this conversation with Edward—I thought, poor Wagner, he must be turning in his grave to think that after so many years, a Palestinian and an Israeli are going to discuss him and his consequences, but I think, in fact, he is having a very good laugh.

QUESTION: In the process of becoming the leading Jewish Wagnerite, conducting in Bayreuth, have you ever felt embittered, angry, or awkward?

DB: Well, first of all, I don't consider myself a leading Wagnerite or the leading Jewish conductor or the leading anything. I don't really think of myself in those terms, and I don't think of certain events as being pivotal or so important. This whole question of Wagner in Israel has followed me in America especially, and in Germany, too, I must say, but especially in America, in a way that is completely out of proportion. It was an act of musical interest on the part of the orchestra that in the end did not take place, and that was all, and now I'm seen as a pioneer of the necessity of playing Wagner in Israel, and it's not like that at all. Personally, I mean I'm sure I don't have to say this, I don't need to conduct Wagner in Israel, if they don't want to hear it. I can conduct my Wagner somewhere else, and yet, I have become a sort of exponent of all these things, which I am not, and I don't consider myself a leading Wagnerite; I don't consider myself a Wagnerite at all. I happen to think that my preoccupation, or occupation, with Wagner's work is something that is musically very important to me and something that is helpful in my development as a musician and in my occupation with other music.

The connotation of what Bayreuth represented is, of course, clear to me, but I think that Bayreuth and the symbolism and the associations of Bayreuth that you are talking about concern the Bayreuth of the thirties, even of the twenties, and of course the forties, but not the Bayreuth since 1951. And I think that one has to be really very clear—and I think as a Jew I can say that—one has to be very clear about how one deals with one's enemies and with the people who hate us and who have hated us over the centuries. You can either come to terms with them or you can continue to have no contact with them, but I'm not in favor of accepting only what is in our favor from them and otherwise criticizing them and having nothing to do with them. I think that if the Israeli government accepted German reparations in the fifties, and if the Israeli government allowed German cars to come to Israel, and all that, it should be possible also to play Wagner for those people who want it played and those people who want to hear it without forcing it on anybody else. My feeling about Bayreuth is that any kind of resentment is more than perfectly justified, and I'm not in any way trying to be insensitive here to the incredible suffering that our people, our Jewish people, have had, but any dealing with the past has to be very clearly defined and very clearly articulated. I don't think that we have any right to have a sort of generalized criticism, if not hatred, of the people who hated us, because then we only descend to the level of those people who persecuted us for so many years.

New York,
October 7, 1995

Chapter Five

⸺◦◦◦⸺

AG: What does authenticity, especially in the more general sense of fidelity to text, mean, and how does this notion translate, if at all, to other arts?

DB: Music is different from the written word because music only exists when the sound is created. When Beethoven wrote the Fifth Symphony, it simply existed as a figment of his imagination and was subject to physical laws that he imagined only in his brain. And then, he used the only known system of notation, which is black spots on white paper. And nobody is going to convince me that these black spots on white paper are the Fifth Symphony. The Fifth Symphony comes into being only when an orchestra, somewhere in the world, decides to play it. Therefore, the peculiarity of music resides in the fact that there's this phenomenon of sound and that music means different things to so many different people, whether it's something poetic, mathematic, or sensual, whatever it is. But in the end, music expresses it only through sound, which is, Busoni says, sonorous air. That's basically all it is. And therefore, when you talk about fidelity, fidelity to what? You're talking about the fidelity of a very approximated, poor system. And if it's written in the score, *piano,* and you play *forte,* then you are obviously unfaithful to the text. We are not talking about that. But I think it's very important to remember that the musical experience, the act of making music, means to bring the sounds into a state of constant interdependency—in other words, that you cannot separate, because the speed is related to the content, to the volume, etc. And therefore, everything is relative and is always connected to what came before, to what came after, and also to what happens simultaneously. When a violinist plays a passage in a Beethoven symphony that is marked *piano*—*piano* in relation to what? In relation to what came before and in relation to what is above or below him at that point. And therefore, you cannot speak of fidelity. And if you try to objectively reproduce what is printed and nothing more, not only is this not possible to do—and, therefore, there's no fidelity—it is also a complete act of cowardice because it means that you haven't gone to the trouble to understand the interrelations and what the dosage is, to speak of nothing else—and I'm speaking at the moment only about volume and about balance, let alone the question of the line and the phrasing and all that.

EWS: And tempo.

DB: Yes, but tempo is the famous parallel. You know, tempo is always related to the content, and many musicians make, to my mind, the fatal mistake of first deciding on a tempo. They take a metronome, sometimes given by the composer, which is inevitably too fast because when the composer writes the metronome marking, he doesn't have the weight of sound. He only has the imagination in his brain. You can recite a poem that you know by heart, and you can recite it in two seconds, but you would never read it aloud in two seconds. And therefore, the metronome marks of composers are inevitably too fast, including a very experienced conductor such as Pierre Boulez. And he put it in a very charming and French way. When I conducted the world premiere of his *Notation VII* and the metronome mark was over 50 percent faster than we were playing it, he was very happy and changed the metronome marking. "How come?" I asked. "You are such an experienced and cerebral"—in the best sense of the word—"musician." He said, "This is very simple. When I compose, I cook with water, and when I conduct, I cook with fire." Anyway, this has led, at least, many musicians simply to take the decision of the tempo as a first decision and, then, see what content you put into it. And you cannot do that. It's exactly the other way. It's the content that really determines the tempo. Obviously, all this is relative, and there's a certain speed that is necessary for a certain content to come to the expression. Take the last movement of the Beethoven Seventh, and instead of playing it fast, relatively fast, or very fast—this is the margin, I think, that we are allowed—we are playing slowly and softly instead of the fast and loud where it is written, so the content will simply not come through. And this is a parallel, which can be found in the political process. No matter what you think of the Oslo Accord—in other words, it had a chance or it didn't have a chance—it lost all chance of succeeding when the tempo, the speed at which it was proceeding, became so slow. The music dissipates when it's so slow, and the process, also, because there is no separation. In music, there is really no separation between the different elements. And these elements cannot be written down. And therefore, fidelity to the text, as such, is very limited. It is, of course, limited to soft, loud, fast, slow, and even those things are relative. But anything other than doing all of that is an act of cowardice. And the interesting thing is that when one talks about fidelity to a text, very often today, one always talks about speed: "Why doesn't so and so take time in such and such a passage?" or "Why does he push the tempo forward?" I mean, *legato* is also a question of fidelity to the text. In other words, we have become so obsessed with this machine of tempo that the content is becoming absolutely separated. And therefore, it is also a victim of this mania that we have toward specialization, in the sense of dissecting elements and making them independent. I don't mind specialization if you are a medical doctor and you specialize in a certain part of the anatomy. I understand that. But it's always in relation to the rest of the body. You cannot be an ear, throat, and nose specialist and not have any idea about the rest of the body, because there are things that are interrelated. And the music is exactly like the human body. The anatomy of music is exactly that: everything is always related. But the minute that one follows the line of specialization in its narrowest and most primitive way, as is so much the fashion today, you find, in the end, that you're dissecting it and are occupying yourself only with one element; and therefore, music-making has no chance to exist in this kind of condition.

AG: You would be very happy to know that in an unrelated conversation with Pierre Boulez, he said two things that are exact parallels to what you are talking about. I asked him how being a performer affected him as a composer, and he said that by being a performer he can never get very far from the tangible reality of producing the sound because otherwise, as you suggested, composing is an abstract art, and it exists to an inner ear. And then, he made a very elaborate analogy, which I'll paraphrase, but it's very Platonic, in that he regarded the score or the composer's intention as a kind of unseen source, and the perception of it is through a series of reflections from the listener's point of view. It's never the source. You never, if you will, quite see the fire or the light. You see a series of mirrors, whether it's from the score to the conductor to the people who produce the actual sound to the audience, or whatever the formula is. And he said: To think as a listener that you are seeing the source is an illusion. What you're seeing is a series of essential reflections.

EWS: It's very interesting. I would like to think more about intention because while it's true to say that there is a kind of inertness and lifelessness to what's on the paper, nonetheless, I think one has to, in the process of interpretation—speaking both from the point of view of an interpreter and somebody who produces work that is interpreted—to hold on to something, whether you call it the original text or whether you want to call it an agreed upon set of conventions, that gives you something to return to. Now it's never, obviously, the pristine material that the composer wrote. You can't get back to that. I want to come back to that idea of a text. I think one can talk about a text and establishing a text. We all depend on that. But the work that editors do, in collating manuscripts, in collating notebooks, or at least giving them a presence so that the interpreter or the reader can return to them, is crucial. I mean, we need that basic kind of work. And we need to know the type of detail provided by Alan Tyson—the Mozart scholar, who established the score by looking at watermarks and knowing that a certain passage belongs to this period and not to that period. That work, I think, is essential. Of course, it doesn't determine what you do when you read it or play it, but I think one really has to bow to the necessity of that kind of editing in establishing a text. Then, what do you do with a text? One could then look at a text in two possible ways. One is to say, "Well, it's all there, and all I do is simply, faithfully, reproduce it." That, of course, is total nonsense, because there's no such thing as faithfully reproducing a text. If you're looking at an eighteenth-century text, then you have to be an eighteenth-century person, which is impossible. In a sense, once a composer or writer has written the text and is, therefore, distant from it, it becomes an object on its own, without the kind of protection that its author thinks it can be given. Nevertheless, I think that we all feel, as interpreters, readers, or, in the case of music, performers, that, in producing a performance or a reading, the text is not an infinitely malleable object. In other words, there are resistances to the interpreter's willfulness in it: *forte, piano,* you know, all kinds of instructions. I think it's important to say that, so it isn't completely open to do or interpret in whatever way one chooses. I mean, we know what a travesty it would be, for example, if somebody decided to put on *King Lear* as a comedy. It's just something basically wrong. Or *Othello* as a farce. It just doesn't work. But I think the best kind of interpretation, therefore, would be to regard the text as the result of a series of decisions made by the composer, writer, or the poet, the result of which we get. And therefore, to read it, one must try to understand the process by which these notes or these words have gained a presence on the paper. And that's a very complicated thing, because, in fact, it involves—Boulez's word is "mirrors"—a series of intuitions, a series of educated guesses in the style, in the discipline of reproducing sound or reproducing words in such a way that gives them a kind of attention-getting novelty when they're heard. Interpretation and performance become boring if the performer or the interpreter simply repeats what other people have done. You want to try and give a new impulse or new shape. But what I think is also extremely important is to understand the interpreter's role not just in the context of the original composer or poet but also of the performer and interpreter in the present. That is to say, we are all constrained by certain conventions that make it impossible for us to go beyond certain norms, and those are, in the end, socially and intellectually determined. So, I think there's a kind of interplay constantly between the individuality of the reader, performer, interpreter, on the one hand, and the whole history of decisions, consensus, and transmission of a text from its history, whether it was five minutes ago or two hundred years ago, that makes it available in the present. And therefore, the interpretive process is a dynamic one, which always requires, I think, a great deal of rational examination and isn't a matter to be determined simply by feeling. Feeling is very important, and you can't, obviously, interpret something that you hate in quite the same way as you would interpret something that you love or care about or think is important. But I think there's always a very disciplined process, which binds us. In other words, there's a kind of convention in the sense of a contract. Do you agree?

DB: Yes. But the element of sound is very different. In other words, when you talk about music, you're not talking about interpretation in the same way that you would talk about the text at all.

EWS: Well, let's talk about that.

DB: I don't think there is a real interpretation of music as such. You have to first start with the physical realization of the sound. You don't talk about the physical realization of the word in a poem.

EWS: No. You wouldn't call it physical realization, but the word I would use would be actualization. If you look at a poem, like this, which has a text, these are words that are completely inert; they mean nothing until you actualize and read them. And then, when you read them, you're realizing them. I would say that is a rough similarity.

DB: Yes, but you don't have to deal with physical laws. With sound, you have to deal with physical laws, where there's the effect of sound in a room, the space and time, all these things. You don't have that as a reader. In other words, the equivalent would be to read a poem or to read a score, but to actually perform it, or even play it at home, involves a physical act that requires a musician to have understanding and knowledge of the physical side of music, which has to do with acoustics, which has to do with overtone, which has to do with harmonic relationship . . .

EWS: And, of course, technique.

DB: But there's a physical aspect. And you cannot get to metaphysics without having gone through physics before. And therefore, this is the singular phenomenon of musical performance. And this is why I believe that the word "interpretation" was misused and understood by many people, I think, in a false way: in other words, "How do I interpret this?" "How do I make it my own?" "How do I make it not only Beethoven but I make it my own?" But you can't. It doesn't really exist that way.

You cannot do that. You have to understand, first of all, the physicality of how the sound of Beethoven's Fifth really operates; and how the orchestra has to be balanced; and how the texture has to be sometimes thick and sometimes thin; what is the speed of the dynamics—in other words, it says *crescendo*; the *crescendo* mark is written vertically through the whole score, but if all the instruments of the orchestra start to *crescendo* at the same time, you don't hear everything. Obviously, the horns, trumpets, and timpani will cover the rest of the orchestra. Therefore, this concept of fidelity to the text in music is much more relative, and relative in the sense not that you're not bound by a contract, as you say, but more relative in the sense that you sin by omission. If you play it, as it were, only as it is written, and not try to understand what it really means, you sin by omission. If, in other words, it says *crescendo* for the whole orchestra and you let, as a conductor, all the instruments go through, you are being faithful to the text, but you sin by omission because you omit many things because they are not heard anymore.

EWS: I wonder whether maybe the interesting parallel might be not from literature to music but from music to literature in the interpretation of the text. In other words, whether one could base oneself on some of the things that you've just said and apply them to the reading of a poem. For instance, you take a poetic line of Keats: "Thou still unravish'd bride of quietness." Well, that's not everyday language. It's not the language we use to make up a laundry list or talk to somebody on the subway. So, in that respect, if one considers poetry as requiring a particular kind of language, then it's figured language, not ordinary prose. The disadvantage, of course, of literature is that it uses a coinage that is to be found interchangeably with everyday usage, which music doesn't. The sonorous material of the Beethoven symphony is not to be found anywhere else, but you can find the verbal material of a Keats poem by walking outside and just listening to people talk, more or less. You could say, as the literary critic Richard Poiriet has said recently, that literature is more democratic, in that everybody can use it. It's the words that we live by, in a way, put to extraordinary use. I would say that it's more profitable to think of it as a form—poetic language or figured language—that comes closer to some aspects of music. Words are normally turned toward a practical purpose or an objective meaning. If we say, "This is a glass," we're trying to signify this object outward. But if you think of a poetic text in the musical sense, what you have is a relationship within the text the way elements relate inside of a score. Everything becomes relative to that usage. It's not just a matter of saying, "Well now, of course I understand what a bride is; I understand what quiet is; and I understand what unravish'd means; therefore, I understand that line." It doesn't work that way because the poetic object is a whole series of relationships, internal to the poem, which you need to understand before you can, if you will, "read" it. So, in that respect, I think the interpretation of a piece of music provides a kind of parallel. But then, there's also the question of what would then be the equivalent of the realization of sound, which is what you've been talking about—the physical quality of the relationship of sound. In that respect, music is unique, quite on its own: both its accessibility and its inaccessibility, at the same time. That's the great paradox, in a way. Obviously in order to hear a Keats poem and to make something of it, you have to know English. But to listen to a piece of music, you don't have to know German, you don't have to know French, even if it's a German piece or a French piece. You have to be tutored, to a certain degree, in the musical style and musical

language. But it's arguable—we know this from actual cases—
that children can understand music without understanding
language. You're a perfect example of that. You could probably
play before you could make consecutive philosophical statements in Spanish. Right? And therefore, the whole question of
accessibility is that, on the one hand, music makes a very powerful immediate effect, as so many philosophers have noted,
and, therefore, is, in a sense, more dangerous because it can
stimulate a certain kind of irrationality, I suppose. Nietzsche
certainly felt that, as did Plato, and so on. But on the other
hand, it is an extremely esoteric art. It requires a kind of training that you might say is a discipline rather like that of a Jesuit.
And in that respect, it becomes very inaccessible. There's
something quite mysterious and esoteric about it. And I think
this is what you're dealing with all the time as a performing
musician.

DB: I want to refer to something you said earlier about the
text. If you look at a play, and you look at an opera, which also
has this theater but has music to it, what are the differences
basically? In the spoken theater, there are no indications of
speed or loudness. This is why so many stage directors that are
very powerful in spoken theater have difficulty with opera
because they feel they are in a straitjacket. They suddenly cannot make the singer shout something because the composer,
in a very uncomfortable way, wrote *pianissimo* there; and the
singer tells him, "I can't shout—it says *pianissimo*." And then,
he has to wait for the next time, because there are suddenly
four bars of orchestral interlude—the preparation for the state
of mind of the singing actor for the next line—something you
don't have in spoken theater. And these are all the very important differences between spoken text and music. It also has to
do with sound. The element of sound is what gives a certain

tragic element to all music. If you really are able to build a phrase with a continuous sound, so that each note follows the preceding note—starts at the level that the preceding note ended and finishes the note at the level that the next note starts—you already have, through this element of sound, an element of tension and an element of something keeping you in midair because, otherwise, it would drop the sound, which means it would drop to the floor. And therefore, without any dynamic, before you even start with all that, there is an element of tension in sound that you simply don't have in words. Another very important point, for me, is that if you study music in the deepest sense of the word—all the relationships, the interdependence of the notes, of the harmonies, of the rhythm, and the connection of all those elements with the speed; if you look at the essential unrepeatability of music, the fact that it is different every time because it comes in a different moment—you learn many things about the world, about nature, about human beings and human relations. And therefore, it is, in many ways, the best school for life, really. And yet, at the same time, it is a means of escape from the world. And it is with this duality of music that we come to the paradox. How is it possible that something that can teach you so much about the world, about nature and the universe, and, for more religious people, about God—that something that is so clearly able to teach you so many things can serve as a means of escape from precisely those things? And this is a fascinating thought, for me, about the effect of music. Whenever we talk about music, we talk about how we are affected by it, not about it itself. In this respect, it is like God. We can't talk about God, or whatever you want to call it, but we can only talk about our reaction to a thing—some people know God exists and others refuse to admit God exists—but we cannot speak about it. We can only speak about our reaction to it. In the same way, I don't think you can speak about music. You can only speak about a subjective reaction to it.

EWS: There is a complete sort of discourse in the history of religion, whether you call it mysticism, Sufism, or whatever, where religious experience is that of the ineffable, the unspoken, the unreachable, the unattainable. It exists certainly in all the monotheistic religions and, to some degree, in some of the pluralistic religions. It's very interesting that, in the case of some composers—one thinks of Messiaen and certainly of Bach—there's an attempt not so much to approach the divine but to embody the divine. Think of mystical language—whether you read Saint John of the Cross or you read Ibn Arabi, who's a great Arabic mystic—there's a fantastically powerful conviction there that interests me—that these are people who are, in effect, giving you the word of God. And they certainly wouldn't say, "Well, it's an approximation to it." They would say, "No. This is God speaking through me." So, I think it's a more powerful phenomenon even than what we've been discussing. It's quite strange, for me anyway, being somebody who is totally not religious. I'm quite secular in that respect. But I'm very drawn to works of that sort, and not only because of the religious element. It's because I keep thinking, in the case of Bach, whose forms are so rationalistic in a way, that the representation of the biblical drama in a staggeringly rich and compelling work like the *Saint Matthew Passion* can be explained by saying, "Well, there must be some actual rational law that explains it." But the work always seems to be moving away from you. I think that's the fascination. Not that you say, "Well, we're only approaching it." You actually feel you're getting closer to it, but it's always drawing away.

DB: I think it's something that has to do with the phenomenon of harmony. In tonal music, it's easier to explain. I've felt similar feelings and thoughts with non-tonal music, but in tonal music, it's very much easier to explain. Take the beginning of the second movement of the Beethoven Fifth Piano Concerto, with its sustained violins and viola and *pizzicato* cello and bass: it is, in a way, very easy to understand why it can have a certain form of divinity to it.

EWS: Or ultimate serenity of some sort.

DB: It's the sense of harmony that is in it—harmony not just in the musical sense but harmony of thought and harmony of feeling. There are many ways to analyze it. You could say it is, of course, on the one hand, the ability for a sustained line of violins and violas to walk slowly and unperturbed, marchlike. This gives you a feeling of great serenity. And the ability for lower sounds plucked by the cellos and double basses which give these sustained lines rhythmic pulsation. And you feel that the whole world is in harmony: the sustained and the plucked; and the long and the short. And there is room for everybody to exist in peaceful coexistence. I'm, obviously, paraphrasing it. But all those things give a feeling of what, I think, people perceive as divinity, which is a feeling of serenity, of tranquility. And then, when you get passages where there is great harmonic tension with chromaticism and unresolved chords, without going as far as *Tristan und Isolde*—in Beethoven, there are many of those, even if it's one note that clashes there—for many people, this is also a feeling that this is a protest that one has against whatever form of almighty or omnipresent force exists above us. So, I think that music has the capacity to do that. And in a way, a piece of music, no matter how short or how long it is, can immediately give you the feeling of having lived through a whole life, even if it is a small Chopin waltz, which lasts only, with the "Minute Waltz," about a minute and a half or so, simply by the mere fact that there was no sound and suddenly there is sound. And then comes the last note and there was sound and is no more, and sometimes you get either naïve or poetic to see that you have lived through something, which has existed and doesn't exist anymore.

AG: Isn't the current sort of fascination with authenticity, which is happily waning, an attempt to rationalize and quantify something that's ultimately unquantifiable and irrational? Richard Taruskin makes this argument: that the idea of authenticity is a very modern thought; that a generation ago, or when Wagner conducted Beethoven, he didn't sit and say, "Oh, my God; let me go back and do it exactly as Beethoven intended."

EWS: No, but he was driven by an idea of authenticity, because he thought, in his own way, he was getting to the true Beethoven, which nobody else understood.

AG: But without the same focus on a measurable, reproducible standard of historical accuracy. For example, he didn't want to worry about the exact number of violins and where they sat.

EWS: No. But that's a different emphasis; it's a different language of the time. He was obsessed with authenticity. What is authenticity?

DB: He wanted authenticity of feeling.

EWS: I know, but authenticity of feeling, he thought, determined the sound in a way. But what *is* authenticity all about? Authenticity is also about justifying the present, you know, in relation to the past. In other words, if I say that this is the authentic, you know, I am also saying that this is the true. Well, in Christianity, people wander around looking for pieces of the true cross. So, it's always about something in the present. It's really misleading to think that authenticity is about the past. It's about the present and of how the present sees and constructs the past and what past it wants; you know, and it's necessary to have this kind of past. Look at the desire for "authenticity" in the performance of eighteenth-century music in the last thirty years. It's all about a reaction to the plush sound of great orchestras, and the purists want these new reedy things grinding away to say, "This is the way Bach really sounded, not the way Furtwängler used to do Bach with the Berlin Philharmonic." So, it's really about a contest in the present over a construction of the past. I would want to emphasize all of it. There's a necessary element of construction. Wouldn't you agree?

DB: I definitely agree. And I think that we talk so often about what kind of future we want for ourselves that we don't occupy ourselves enough with the question of what past we want. And this is at the core of the problems for Germans of the second half of the twentieth century and now in the beginning of the twenty-first century. What kind of a past do they want to really have, as far as this dark period of the Nazi time? It is a question that will occupy Americans, vis-à-vis Vietnam, that will occupy Israelis vis-à-vis Palestinians, and Palestinians vis-à-vis

Israelis. If you look at the world this way, you see that fidelity is also a very, very relative concept—fidelity of text or fidelity of interpretation; and why it is that certain events in history seem in a certain way at one moment and, twenty or thirty years later, completely different. The event is already long gone, and yet it influences the development of history in a different way. I think the movement of authentic practice in music that we have seen over the last thirty or forty years has many advantages. It has brought to the fore the path, the progress, of articulation much more so than before. And this is the aspect of it that interests me much more than whether they play with four violins, because there are a lot of inconsistencies. Why should you play with four or six violins in a hall that seats two thousand people? You can do that if you play it in a room the size of the rooms where the works were played in the eighteenth century. I have a great philosophical problem with the movement of period performance practice.

If we accept Edward's assumption that it is a picture of the present, then it shows a very poor picture of the present, because there has never been a generation so preoccupied with the past as now. In archeology you see how cities were built on top of others. We don't have the courage to leave behind the things that have to be left behind and go on. This, for me, is part of the illness of society today. And the difference between the authentic movement today and Schumann or Mendelssohn or Wagner playing Bach and Beethoven is that they were really modern. They were trying to bring the past to their time. And there is an assumption, which I think is a presumption, on the part of many members of this movement today, that assumes that this is a very modern trend, whereas, in fact, it is really only trying to go back because of the lack of ability to transform it into something contemporary. What I'm trying to say by this is that the Liszt arrangements of Bach for the piano brought Bach to the nineteenth century, so that the sound was something similar to what people were hearing, in those days, from Liszt's own composition. There is a lot to be gained from musical scholarship. To understand the style, understand intimately all the different elements that are part of this music, is, of course, absolutely necessary and is of interest, *sine qua non*. But to try and reproduce the past? The mere word "reproduce" is already a sign of poverty.

AG: That's a very good distinction.

EWS: There's an analogy for it, in the literary world, an analogy which I think takes a quite narrow view of history. It's a similar thing to hear these people who say that we have to return to the classics; that students today are not reading enough of Homer, Virgil, and so on. They say this not because they're interested so much in Homer and Virgil, but, as I tried to suggest earlier, because they want to use Homer and Virgil as a way of beating down contemporary literature, contemporary concerns that are disturbing (i.e., gender, race, class, etc.). They argue that we have lost touch with our national heritage—the essentially European Judeo-Christian civilization—and we should spend our time reading more of these authentic masters of the past. Let's not waste our time with women's literature, black literature, ethnic literature, and all that sort of thing.

Now, what's that about? Most of the people who advocate this view advance no real ideas about the works, except to say that they should be read, that Dante and Virgil should be read. And who would disagree with that? Virgil *should* be read. But it doesn't mean that in reading Virgil, you should stop reading everything else. Allan Bloom actually says we should stop reading everything after Nietzsche, and we should really spend our time reading basically the Greek philosophers, a couple of poets, and the French Enlightenment writers, and that education is all about an elite, really. Not everybody should be educated. If you excavate a bit more in this whole question of authenticity and the past, you again come upon the question of the "other." What is involved there, of course, are issues in the present but also a question of who is entitled to the past. There's a kind of snobbery that is also very evident in the whole musical authenticity movement.

AG: There, the question of entitlement has become literal. We seem to be coming out of it, but there was a time when you weren't entitled to play Bach with the Chicago Symphony any longer.

EWS: Yes. Purists say that this is something that only specialists should do.

DB: But I think that's the most negative effect of this archconservative over-preoccupation with the past.

EWS: It's fundamentalism.

DB: Fundamentalism, preoccupation with the past in literature and music—in that respect, there is absolutely no difference. By knowing your Boulez and your Carter, you see aspects of Beethoven in a different way. And this is what makes Beethoven eternal. And this is why we occupy ourselves with Beethoven today, and not so much with a minor contemporary of his such as John Field, who had much less to say as far as the eternal values of music or ways of expression of music. And we occupy ourselves with Mozart and we don't occupy ourselves with Salieri so much. But also, it is absolutely essential for a musician or a performer to be in constant touch with the music of today in order to understand also the newness of the music of the past. I remember when I conducted the world premiere of *Exody* of Harrison Birtwistle—a very major, long piece—on the same program with the Tchaikovsky *Pathétique* Symphony, I was coming into contact with new sounds that were unknown to me. Obviously, as it was a world premiere, they were unknown to everybody. When you come in touch with that, your instinct or intuition for the newness of sound is much sharper. And I was made aware of so many aspects of the Tchaikovsky symphony in that context. I was able to feel and understand much more the newness of so many passages in the Tchaikovsky symphony. And this is why it's absolutely essential. And of course, as you say, unarguably, that one should read Virgil, but you also have to read today's writers. You have to read some Rushdie or another contemporary author in order to see Virgil in a different way.

EWS: Music presents a particular problem I'd like to address. I think the argument to be made is an interesting one: that, of all the arts, less is known about music today by people in the general culture. In other words, an educated person, who's a philosopher, would be interested in literature, would know a great deal about photography, would know a lot about the cinema, painting, sculpture, theater, and yet would know nothing about music. There's a kind of apartheid which involves music, which I think is unique to this time. Music has always occupied a place that was central to the society, certainly through the nineteenth century, at least in the West.

DB: There were always people who were either insensitive or uninterested; Spinoza was totally uninterested.

EWS: Yes, of course, there are individuals. But by and large, you could say that, in an educated household—let's say, of the middle class, and certainly of the aristocracy, but increasingly the middle class after the French Revolution—music was one of the arts in the full sense of the word. It was part of the currency of literate and intellectual discourse. That's no longer the case. I'm curious to know what you're feeling about it as a performer. My sense of it is that you have two audiences. You have the audience of the sort of people who make it work, which are the corporate and the wealthy people. And my impression is that they tend to be extremely conservative. They don't want new music. They just want endless programs of Mozart, and even Salieri, rather than a retrospective or a program of Birtwistle's music. So that's one issue. The other audience is very small because it is made up of the declining number of people who know music and made it a part of their lives. And a related issue, I think, is the Adorno question. Adorno says that what happened to music is that music becomes, instead of a representation of society, let's say, in Beethoven—the triumphant bourgeoisie, as you see in the trumpet call of *Fidelio*—by the time you get to Schoenberg and the dodecaphonic system, that that is a representation of the inability of music to function within the society. The true new music is the music that cannot be performed and cannot be heard. He actually says that: looking at it the way he looks at it—as a philosophical evolution out of what came before; music as a kind of philosophy of the society—that the reason it's become so difficult and inaccessible is that it represents a kind of ossification of the society, which makes it completely impossible

(a) to perform, (b) to understand, and (c) to listen to. So, I wonder whether there's something of that dialectic that we have to deal with today, leaving aside the question of sponsorship and patrons who want to hear and want things packaged in a particular way. But I wonder whether you feel, as a performer, that if you look at the history of music, evolving, say, out of Wagner into Schoenberg and then Berg and then Webern and then into Carter finally, whether we're not also talking about an increasing sense of difficulty. That is to say, do you not feel in your own work as a performer and organizer of performances, that there is a gradual separation between music and society, and that, in some way, you're trying to compensate by making this music available? In a sense, you're going against the grain of music, you're betraying it by domesticating it too much, by putting on a program somebody like Carter, who's really not meant to be listened to the way one listens to Mozart and Haydn.

DB: Why not?

EWS: Well, because the music of Mozart and Haydn was part of the currency of consumption of that time. And you could look at music as occupying a very different social status. It was a language that was like Latin. One learned it and one used it, whereas today it seems to me the language of music is very highly specialized and designed not to be used or known except by other musical experts, much more so than the music of the time up through the nineteenth century, which is the core repertory of classical music today. I'm just wondering how far one can take the Adornian argument: that the significance of music is that, by the very fact of its bristly complexity, it is an indictment of the inhumanity of a society that forces it to play the role of the great opposite of the society—a society which is all about consumerism and commodification, on the one hand, and about inhumanity, on the other. The inheritors of Schoenberg would have to be caught in this dialectic. Elliott Carter would be one of them. I don't think Messiaen is because Messiaen thought of himself as actually doing something quite different. But in the line of pure modernist music, of which Carter is the great bearer today—probably also Boulez, although Boulez has a very heavy admixture of literary materials in his sound—is there a fundamental contradiction or parallel?

DB: Why does Wagner mark such a critical juncture in music? Why is there always the question of what happened "after Wagner"? There's one overriding answer: the loss of tonality. With the loss of tonality, there is the loss of a certain dimension of music, which is not possible without harmony. There was a musical language and a kind of rational consensus that existed for generations from Bach until Wagner, then it's no longer there. It's as if it went out of existence. There is an element in Wagner's music that reminds me of this very banal Jewish joke: "Why do the Jews always answer a question with another question"; and the answer then, of course, is, "Why not?" It's exactly the principle of *Tristan,* which depends on the lack of resolution, always bringing up another question. It is basically the same core. But it is the principle of tension and release of tension that disappears when tonality disappears, and you have to create other means, in some ways more artificial. This is not meant to say that music that is not tonal is not expressive. On the contrary, there are many masterpieces, such as *Wozzeck.* In the music of the Classical period, you expect a natural order, a natural sequence of tension and release. And therefore, when you have a dominant chord, you know that will release into the tonic. And when the First Symphony of Beethoven was originally played, it was a terrible shock because it started with the dominant seventh chord *not* of C (which is the tonic in C major) but of F (which is the fourth degree or subdominant of C major). The shock was not the fact that it was a dynamic shock or rhythmic shock but that it was a harmonic shock. This is why I find the authenticity movement sometimes very one-sided because they try to reproduce the shock of the actual sound, but it's actually the harmony which is the determinant in this sense of shock. And this, of course, is then gone when tonality disappears. On the other hand, a major factor in the question of accessibility or inaccessibility was that the music of Schoenberg and Berg was so difficult to digest in the 1950s and 1960s because the performances were not of a high enough level. They didn't have the transparency they have now. When you now hear the Chicago Symphony play the Five Pieces of Schoenberg, you basically hear everything; you hear the transparency with a naturalness. In other words, this music also needs time. It is a perfect example that familiarity does not necessarily breed contempt. And the problem with contemporary music and the contemptuous attitude to contemporary music is that, in this case, contempt breeds unfamiliarity, in a very strange way. I know it's a play of words, but it really is that way, because if you have contempt for something, you will never get familiar with it. And so, familiarity is very much attached and linked to accessibility or the lack thereof. And one simply has to have the patience not only to let time evolve but to repeat the pieces that one considers important, until with further and further hearings, they become more accessible.

EWS: Well, that may be true. I'm not so sure about it, though. In other words, I think what you're not giving enough weight to is something within the history and evolution of music, which is that there's a kind of built-in or desired alienation. Thus, I'm not sure exactly that somebody like Elliott Carter would want to be too accessible, because what are the forms of accessibility in our society? Packaged music that you hear on the elevator; discs, which allow you basically to listen to anything you want and in any order without consideration for its structure, without consideration for its context, for its history, for its language. I share your admiration and interest in some of the great present-day masters like Boulez or Birtwistle, but I would say that there's something in the music itself that is designed not to be too easily understood.

DB: But I think there's that same element in late Beethoven.

EWS: That's why Adorno makes such a thing of late Beethoven; for him, late Beethoven is really the presagement of the alienated music of Schoenberg and, I suppose, the other contemporary masters that we're talking about—in other words, that they are meant to be composed in a different and intransigent way. What are some of the characteristics of late Beethoven? Well, late Beethoven defies synthesis. Some of the pieces, like the last sonata, are unfinished; it's only two movements. It defies some of the expectations. There are strangely jarring and abrupt episodes in it. In the opening of the Piano Sonata, Op. 110, you have a very conventional accompaniment, with its melody, sitting next to a fugue, a very complex school piece, in a way. Certainly in the *Hammerklavier* Sonata, you have strange unmotivated trills or unison writing with extraordinarily elaborate and complex fugal passages, which suggests that Beethoven wasn't trying to synthesize them the way he did the fugal passages in the *Eroica*.

DB: And there's also an element of constant interruption.

EWS: It's episodic, fragmentary, unassimilated, and designed that way.

AG: But is it any less communicative for that? Or does it desire to communicate less?

EWS: It's less accessible and, therefore, less about communication. It's not seductive in the same way. It's not meant to address or draw in people. There are, of course, exceptions: obviously, the last movement of the Ninth is meant to be communicative. In a certain way, that's why it's also taken away.

DB: I don't mean to be disrespectful, but I think all this is not so important: accessibility and inaccessibility. Because there has been great music in the past that was great music and was inaccessible, like late Beethoven. Early Bartók was, even in my youth, inaccessible. I played Bartók's First Piano Concerto in the sixties; it was considered very inaccessible. And there's great music that was accessible from the beginning. And therefore, I don't think that the greatness of music is necessarily tied to its accessibility.

EWS: No, it's not. I'm not talking about accessibility. I'm talking about music that has been, in a sense, re-conceived as a mass phenomenon. That is to say, you do have music today, but it's not classical music. The music that dominates today is rock, world music, hip-hop, all those other forms. Those are the forms that dominate the ear, plus the commodified and packaged music. All I'm simply saying is: Do you want to accept this split? This must be difficult for you to think about because you're in it, you do it.

DB: It's not difficult for me, because basically I play or conduct the music that I really want to do, because it interests me, because it fascinates me, and I also want to share it with people. But what you are basically saying is that music today is a protest against society.

EWS: I'm asking.

DB: But I think this was very often the case. I think of Wagner, but also, obviously, of Schoenberg and Stravinsky in many ways. I think there is something to what Edward is trying to say. We live in a more and more political world. The difference between an artist and a politician—not a statesman, in fact, but a politician—is that an artist, to be true to himself, has to have the courage to be totally uncompromising; and the politician, to be true to himself, has to have the art of compromising at the tip of his fingers; otherwise, he's not a politician. And therefore, to be an artist in a political society is to go against the mainstream.

EWS: My impression is that music is losing its authority. I'm simply saying that the kind of speculation that we're interested in and that we've been discussing here is less likely to occur, so far as music is concerned, in the general culture than it was a hundred years ago. And I'm puzzled and dismayed by it.

New York,
December 15, 2000

Chapter Six

❧

AG: This conversation is taking place while we are in the midst of a complete cycle of the Beethoven symphonies and piano concertos with Daniel and the Staatskapelle Berlin. I'm very much struck by how different the experience is of the Beethoven symphonies and the concertos as a cycle, rather than how we normally experience it, which is isolated performances of the pieces or even an isolated all-Beethoven concert, but without the much larger context. What does performing and examining these works as a totality mean to each of you?

DB: I believe very much in cyclical thinking because each work of the composer, or writer, complements the next one. They don't stand as disconnected entities. But this is especially so in the case of Beethoven, where almost every symphony has another idiom. I think that the cycle of Beethoven symphonies is more important, in this way, than a cycle of the Mozart symphonies or the Brahms symphonies or, for that matter, the Bruckner symphonies. Although they're all masterpieces, with every symphony it is as if Beethoven's really found a new idiom, a new harmonic idiom, a new formal idiom, and a new idiom of rhythmic value. Therefore, the whole psychological climate of each piece is entirely different. When you think of the Fourth and the Fifth Symphonies, or you think of the Sixth and the Seventh, which come very close together, they could each be composed almost by a different composer, although they have something very similar. And added to that, there is, of course, the effect of accumulation in a cycle and what the mind remembers from the previous symphony, which makes you play the next one—and I think for the listener too, makes you listen to the next one—in a different way. Intelligence, for me, basically manifests itself in two elements: one is a curiosity about what you've heard and the second is the ability to deduce from one into the other. And therefore, when you listen to the *Pastoral* and then you listen to the Seventh, there are new elements that are deduced from the Sixth and go into the Seventh, which the Seventh would not have had it been played on its own.

EWS: Experiencing this cycle—both the symphonies and the concertos—is very rare, considering how popular Beethoven is. Of course, you get an insight, as Daniel was saying, into the workings of the composer's mind and life. Add to that the insights we get into the performer's mind and you realize that what is unfolding here is far more than discrete performances of individual works. And the first thing that struck me, especially in the performances of the middle works, like the First Concerto and the Eighth Symphony, which is the most recent thing that we've heard, is that there is, in Daniel's performances, an extraordinary animation of everything. It's not as if you get a big sweep that some conductors try for and then the details are left to take care of themselves. I was particularly interested in the interplay between each of the individual parts and how the dialectic between the parts animates an unfolding whole. In other words, you never lose awareness that here was something that was organically connected, not only to the parts of that work but also to parts of other works. You could hear, for example in the Fifth's opening idea, anticipations of the Ninth Symphony and echoes going back. But there was another dialectic, which I found very interesting. The works are not being performed numerically, except for the concertos. In other words, the symphonies go back and forth out of chronological order. And then, of course, a listener has accumulated memories of other performances that one has heard by you and many others. So, it's a fantastically rich experience, which is, in fact, an experience in organizing, re-organizing, disorganizing, and organizing sound again. Sound is no longer just linear but also horizontal, diagonal, top to bottom, bottom to top, middle to forward, middle backwards, and then across pieces, in such a way as to create, in effect, a new whole—the meaning of which is paradoxically withheld. In other words, you can't really say, "This is what it means," because the performance is so all-encompassing that it fills up real time in which it takes place. And then, what you're left with is an attempt at retrospection to try to say, "Well, this is what it means," but then, you realize that all you're left with are approximations. And in a sense, it's the most perfect realization of the interpreter's dilemma: that all interpretations come after the fact and are necessarily, then, lacking in something. You're left, in a sense, with allegory. You could say, "Well, this is really a revelation of a second period in a composer's life," but you're left with the unending challenge of trying to relate that to something beyond itself. And there's the difficulty. I mean, for me, I was struck by the contrast between the intensity of the experience and the social occasion. There's quite a gulf between what's happening on the stage and what's happening in the audience. It takes a significant time-consuming organizational, commercial effort to put together a week of such intellectual and aesthetic consequence, which is, in the end, quite amazingly unlike anything else we might have done during that week.

DB: But the fact that there is such a gulf between the audience and the value of the music has to do with the fact that, for half a century now, music education has practically ceased to exist. And therefore, people really don't know what a Beethoven symphony is. In other words, they, unfortunately, go to hear the *Eroica* because they know if it's a famous symphony by a famous composer, maybe they can hum the tune. But I think that the actual human value and enormous strength of these works is because they were imbued with every intellectual and physical force that Beethoven had. And all the musicological research in the world does not basically alter the fact that these masterpieces are his blood, flesh, and bones.

EWS: I think Beethoven's music, and particularly this fantastic *Choral* Symphony, is all about a certain kind of affirmation, which has a very, very powerful urgent connection to the social affirmation of the human being in a society, with promises of fulfillment, of liberation, and brotherhood. In other words, all the positive things we want to say about human existence are, in a sense, contained, not explicitly, except in the last movement, but implicitly in this fantastic stream of pulsating, organically connected music, which seems to say, "The human adventure is worth it in some way." Right? And at the same time, in the last works, you know, he's teetering on the edge. Those great middle works, the essence of what you're really doing in that cycle, are about affirmation. But they also point you toward the later stage, where the whole question of affirmation and communication has become very problematic. It becomes very mysterious in all the late works. And I think that symbolizes the moment when music really moves out of the world of everyday exertion, of effort, of human solidarity and struggle, into a new realm, which symbolizes the obscurity of music to contemporary audiences today. In other words, music becomes a highly specialized art.

AG: Edward has written eloquently about Adorno and this idea that Beethoven moves from music of the social realm to the purely aesthetic realm in the transfer from the middle works to the late works; although ironically, the Ninth Symphony, which is maybe the most social piece, is a late work. So, it's not even a clean chronology. And music goes from a kind of social statement and a statement of philosophical ideals, as you just articulated, to a very private state. This is a critical change in musical thinking, one that hugely influenced the following generations of composers. Daniel, do you agree with that premise? And I suppose the contrast is the late quartets and the late piano sonatas, as opposed to public utterances.

DB: I'm not sure I agree with it. I think it has to do very much with the individual personality of the composer. I think that there are some musicians who are wonderful musicians—this is certainly not a judgment of their quality—for whom music is a very important part of their lives. And there are others who basically live in music. And again, we come back to the paradox. You can only live in music, as it were, if you have other interests, if you see the parallels with literature, if you see the parallels with painting, if you see the parallel with the development of political processes, and if you have an interest, and then you have the ability to deduce, then all this becomes part of your innermost being; and this comes out in the music; and, therefore, music really becomes your life. And it's not something that you do because you like it, or because you enjoy it, or because it is even important to you. Beethoven was not a communicator in the sense that he wanted to communicate and used music for that. I think Beethoven's greatness stems from the fact that he was completely a musician, and by "completely," I mean I believe firmly that he ate, slept, and drank music throughout his life. I think the fact that he was such a moral person, had such high moral ideas, and that this became part of him and came in the music, does not make the music in itself moral. The proof for that is that it was used by the Nazis. The moment a composer like Beethoven has actually finished writing a piece, that piece becomes independent of him. It becomes part of the world. The qualities that he has put in don't necessarily stay there. So, they can be interpreted or misinterpreted, used or abused, as we have seen in the different political trends, too. But I believe there is an intrinsic moral. Why? Because I believe that the struggle is an essential, integral part of the expression in Beethoven's music. If you don't feel the struggle to get the intensity of the sound—if you're able to produce the sound in a lighthearted, athletic way—it cannot have the intensity. And this applies as much to the soft playing—to the *dolce espressivo* of Beethoven, or the slow movement in the Fourth Symphony, for instance—as it does to the heroic gestures of the Fifth Symphony or the *Eroica:* this element of struggle. Beethoven was really the first composer who used the effect of a very long *crescendo* and then a *subito piano,* a drop in the dynamic. It requires a lot of courage and energy to really go with the *crescendo* to the end, as if you're getting to the precipice and then stop short. The easy way out is, toward the end, to let the energy go. And the same thing when it goes from the *crescendo* into a big *fortissimo*. This is the most difficult thing—to have control of the *crescendo,* the gradual build-up, so that there is enough left for the end. This is really Samson, you know, in the temple opening his arms. And it's much easier to make a *crescendo* in such a way that when one gets near the *fortissimo,* one doesn't always notice the lack of the last impetus and the last drop. It's like when you squeeze an orange. You know, the last drop is the hardest. It's the same thing with the sound. And this is why I think that this element of courage and of struggle are an integral part of performing Beethoven.

AG: You've just described, in purely musical performance terms, what Edward just described, which is this progress against resistance, toward affirmation.

EWS: But that's why I would then remove the word "morality." It's not moral. What you're describing has to do with ethics. Ethics in the sense of a practice that is guided by a moral goal, which is the fullest realization of what is contained in the music. What you described is not the content, which makes people feel good, and so on and so forth, but rather the practice of performing. I mean, this is where authentic performance and true interpretation manifest themselves, in that you follow the logic of Beethoven's struggle in your own performance of it. And that struggle has an ethical meaning insofar as it is a process of sound—constantly moving, constantly dynamic, constantly dialectically informed—in which the performer, in paying attention to Beethoven, to the shape of the effort, is producing the sound that Beethoven had in mind. In other words, you're trying to capture Beethoven's intentions in writing something. When you read the score—the *Eroica* or the Fourth, for example—you imagine what Beethoven had in mind as he was writing it. It's not something you could say like, "Well, what he had in mind was a story of a knight going off to do battle." It's not that at all. It's totally musical. But there's a kind of an argument to it, which you are trying to produce. The ethics of a performance is that you stick to that and don't let go of it or go for the easy thing, where you get a *fortissimo* as a kind of a burst rather than a *fortissimo* as the result of a very, very carefully calibrated process, at the end of which is a certain moment.

DB: But this is one of the difficult things with this music today because the ethic of musicians is one of professionalism. It's not an ethic of conflict. In other words, people forget that when the *Eroica* was first performed, there was no such thing as being a professional orchestral musician. But now, it's become part of the social system, and it is absolutely right that musicians should have full-time employment and a guarantee of work fifty-two weeks a year, and they should be as well paid as possible. I'm all in favor of that. But this must not influence the ethic of the actual music-making. You know, it's simply not good enough. It's not ethical to make a *crescendo* only with your brain; your whole body has to be involved in that. And this is more and more difficult for people to realize, because life in the twentieth and now twenty-first century, in that respect, is very different. And as far as these values are concerned, less good.

EWS: But don't you think a lot of it has to do with professionalism as specialization. In other words, many musicians think of what they're doing as their specialty. And therefore, to them, it's a way of earning a living, you know, as opposed to inhabiting the ethical realm.

DB: Yes, but the ethic I'm talking about is music as a way of life and the professional thing is music as a means of life. This is actually the main difference: the way of life and the means of life.

EWS: So, there's a kind of commitment in music-making that you're talking about, which is not necessarily present all the time.

DB: And this is what extraordinarily comes naturally, in my experience, only to the Staatskapelle Berlin.

EWS: Why? I'm curious about that, because you've conducted every orchestra.

DB: Actually, one cannot talk about music as one talks about sports: the best or the worst. And I'm not saying that this is the best orchestra in the world. There are other very fine orchestras, too. But this orchestra has a natural way of standing in front of this music with a mixture of a sense of awe and a great sense of active courage. These are two things that don't often go hand in hand: a sense of awe and courage. A sense of awe, very often, brings human beings to a level of fear and inactivity; and courage, very often, brings human beings to extremes of, I would say, almost self-gratification—through the act of courage that you cannot have a sense of awe. And we always come to the same point of paradox as being, for me, really one of the essential elements to understand life. But it's very difficult to achieve that because it seems a parallel. But when you get, on the one hand, a sense of awe, which is passive, and, on the other side, the courage to do, which is active, you get this fantastic intensity. I believe that this orchestra has this quality for several reasons. One has to do with the fact that they lived under a totalitarian regime, basically, for sixty years: from 1930 through the Nazis and then the Communists in East Germany. This certainly does not justify the need for a totalitarian regime. But music and culture, in general, has very often much greater importance in daily life under a totalitarian regime. The worst of that regime is that it made people live in constant fear. There was an element of mistrust that was necessary for the regime to continue: mistrust between friends, between families, etc.; so that when these musicians went to play the concerts or the operas in the Staatsoper, they were really able to breathe and be free. And those who were against the regime felt that music was like a kind of oxygen, because this was the one place where they could really be free. And those musicians who were in favor of the regime were only too proud that such a wonderful institution existed under such a regime. Therefore, from both sides, you had a different attitude to the profession.

AG: There's a much greater urgency to the existence of an orchestra in such circumstances.

DB: It has nothing to do with making a living.

AG: In a way, it's the opposite of professionalism as an idea.

DB: Absolutely. It is exactly the opposite. This is the paradox. And add to that the very solid and deep—in that respect, old-fashioned—musical education of Germany, with a much greater preoccupation with harmony and structure, and much less so with individual virtuosity of the instrument. And what makes this orchestra's Beethoven so special is that, first of all, most of them imagine the sound that they want to hear before they play it, in a very similar way, which has nothing to do with the individual quality of playing. This comes on top of it. But you cannot get eighty or ninety musicians, who all play very well but who each have different ideas of the sound, to play with this kind of homogeneity and, therefore, with this kind of inner strength. For this, you need them all to be able to imagine the sound in a very similar way. The combination of these two factors—the attitude to the profession beyond the professional and the fact that they have such a thorough musical education—makes each one of them play from the score and not from their part. By this, I mean that wherever they play, they are perfectly and consciously aware of what this note that they are playing at that moment actually means in the context. In other words, what is the place of that note: what is the place of that note in the chord; and what is it both vertically and horizontally. And this is a very important factor in music-making, what one would call the vertical pressure of the horizontal discourse. This means that the melodic line and the rhythm go in a horizontal direction, but there is always a vertical pressure of the chording, of the harmonies, that is constantly there. In this respect, music is exactly like history, which has to be lived both simultaneously and subsequently.

EWS: This wholeness, this structural wholeness, as you described it, the education of the musicians and the way they play in the case of the Staatskapelle, and particularly in Beethoven, is disappearing throughout our society. If you think of the major pressures, intellectual and social, that exist, they are toward greater pragmatism—in other words, specialization of knowledge, so that only fellow experts can understand each other. The moment you step out of a particular field, you can no longer communicate with anyone else. The other day, I gave a lecture at the medical school. I talked about late style, for instance, and someone said, "You know, you talked about music; you talked about literature; that doesn't go on in our world, in the world of the natural sciences or of medicine." I said, "Why?" He said, "Because I'm a neurobiologist. I can only talk to other neurobiologists." The idea of a common discourse doesn't exist anymore because, first of all, our training is extremely specialized, and then, the whole funding apparatus is geared toward the fragmentation of knowledge, so that people do more and more about less and less. Maybe it's a good thing in the sciences, but there is a certain kind of ideological indoctrination that more or less says, "Well, it's not your problem; somebody else will solve it for you; you're no longer responsible for that." There is a sense, particularly in the United States, that we don't need to know about the rest of the world. The awareness of the overall society and the destiny of where we are going, whether it concerns the environment, the arts, or history, is diminished. For example, in America, history is considered to be what is forgotten. When you say to someone "you're history," it doesn't mean that you're a part of it; it means that you're obliterated. *That*'s what history means. Therefore, what you've described as the ethos of music-making, in the case of the Staatskapelle and the case of Beethoven, is a kind of utopian whole, the sense of which is rapidly being lost elsewhere. People are no longer educated that way in music, and certainly not in literature. I know because I've been teaching for forty years, and I realize now that young students know less and less. You could take for granted, when I began, that students had been educated, first of all, in languages. Everybody was required to know at least two other languages. As a teacher, you could assume that they knew there was a body of literature, let's say, in English or French, which began in such and such a way that included great figures like Milton and Shakespeare and Wordsworth and Yeats, and so on. You can't assume that anymore. There's a kind of a pursuit of the narrow, the particular, and the specialized. And the result is that there's a kind of overall battle where it's very difficult, in discourse or in intellectual exchange, to have the kind of illuminating and liberating moments that your performances of Beethoven this week afford us. Do you understand what I'm trying to say? To me, it seems to be a much more important thing than the performance of a piece.

DB: Of course.

EWS: And it, therefore, supplies a kind of implicit sort of lack in the rest of the social climate, which is, I think, deeply threatening.

AG: Isn't, in Beethoven—actually to use your phrase and turn it slightly—the ideal of a common discourse one of the most powerful driving forces?

DB: Yes, of course. "Alle Menschen werden Brüder."

AG: It's given specific voice in the Ninth Symphony, but it's implicit in so many other places.

EWS: Adorno says the symbol of that is the trumpet call in *Fidelio*. Everything converges at that moment. Florestan is about to be killed. He's saved. Fidelio reveals herself, so that what is hidden becomes open, clear in the light of day. Pizarro's defeated. And Fernando arrives. It's a unique moment of transformation—of catharsis from a true crisis, where everything is threatened with extinction, to the appearance of liberation, light, and C major, with which the opera ends. As a performer, you live the life of the ecstasies of performance; but then, there's the aftermath. I wonder in the case here that you're describing, whether this paradox of performance versus aftermath is deeper now than it was when you began to perform fifty years ago. Do you feel that more?

DB: Yes. Because I feel that the element of professionalism and the element of commercialism in our world have changed that. From my point of view, neither of those elements is, like most things in life, only good or bad. But the abyss is greater and greater. And I think that the fact that so many millions of people live—I think maybe, in some way, in the United States more so than in Europe—totally removed from everything that is outside, has been made even more dramatically obvious since the end of the Cold War. First of all, you do not have the element of fear about the other side, nor is there the element of the good versus the bad, which was felt by both sides in opposite directions. And now that this problem has been solved, I think that there is a sort of quiet underlying sense of triumph in American thinking about the development of the world. You can now say, "Well, we overcame the last hurdle of the battle against Communism and for freedom, and now, we can live on." But I think that the element of dramatic struggle, as there is in Beethoven—in other words, the first subject being more heroic or more masculine, and the second being more gentle or more feminine or whatever you want to call it; and how the two are put in constant juxtaposition—this is something that is required in daily life from everybody. In the same way that there is a certain element of femininity in every masculine human being, and vice versa—this is accepted sexually; it is accepted emotionally; but the same thing has to be part of the political system; and that unless you have the opposite, you cannot really fulfill yourself. And this is what frightens me more than anything since the end of the Cold War, that there isn't that anymore.

EWS: Well, but it exists in other ways. Take, for example, both in Europe and in the United States, the whole question of immigration. You live in Germany, which has a vast non-German population. Look at the emergence of Haider in Austria. There's a kind of xenophobia, which causes people with this sense of triumph and isolationism to say, "Well, you know, we want to preserve what we have and to keep it pure." I think that's a real fear. It exists in this country too. In other words, there is an uneasy sense that America should be homogenized, and that there are these "other" people out there—whether you call them Mexicans or blacks or Africans, and so on—that either have to be kept at bay or absorbed. In other words, there isn't a healthy exchange between self and "other." I think that's disappearing. Either everything is absorbed into this one kind of monochromatic, homogenous, mindless whole or there's an active sense of the classic civilization threatened by new forces, the response to which is often, "We have to be careful about the other; the other is dangerous." And I think that the real problem today is that there's no mediation between these two extremes. Either there's homogenization or there is xenophobia, but not the sense of exchange. It's taking place in many parts of the world. Hence the need to return to origins: you know, people who say, "Let us go back to roots"; the need to find the German past, the Jewish past, the Arab past, the

American past. There is a need to find a past that's uncontaminated by anything, even though it's completely unhistorical, because the past is very much like the present.

DB: Germany has not historically been a country of immigration like the United States or like Argentina, where I was born. But Germany became a country of immigration only through the collective bad conscience in the aftermath of the Nazi period.

EWS: Wasn't it also because they needed cheap labor?

DB: A combination of both. They were unable to say, "We don't want non-Germans," after what happened with the Nazis. The world would never have tolerated that. And therefore, all the non-Aryan immigrants in Germany came, as it were, unnoticed, and suddenly, there were too many of them. So there is an element of justified discussion about how open the borders have to be and what they want to do. Some immigrants have become a very helpful, organic, and positive part of German society, but others have not. They try to impose their habits and religious culture habits on the whole surroundings, and Germans rebel against that. And it does not have the inner structure of the United States, where there's a tradition of Jewish immigration, Italian immigration, the Polish, the Arab. You know, throughout the twentieth century, this has become absolutely natural—you can be Polish and American; and you can be Arab and American; you can be Jewish and American. Well, you can't be Turkish and German in Germany yet. It will take time. And therefore, there are a lot of people who fight against that. And I think that this peculiarity of German thought and German being, when taken in the wrong direction, leads inevitably to Fascist thinking. Musically speaking, I have no problem with the fact that so many people felt, in the twentieth century, that there was a German way of playing, a German kind of phrasing, and a German way of creating sound. It becomes Fascist only when they started saying that only a German can really understand and feel that. And now, in today's world, we are often given the choice between a sort of globalization—everybody is the same, everybody sounds the same—or some kind of Fascist preservation of unique national value. And both are wrong. What is wonderful about this German sound—as it is of the French sound or the Italian sound—is that it can be understood, felt, and expressed by anyone. I mean the best proof of that is that you have so many great musicians from countries where this music doesn't exist. Like from India in Zubin Mehta's case, or from Japan in the case of so many wonderful musicians. At the risk of sounding arrogant, I must say Argentina is not exactly a country that produced so much great music, so many great composers, and yet I am able to conduct and play the great German repertoire because I try to penetrate the German musical tradition.

EWS: It's a very interesting problem, actually. It seems to me that the basic humanistic mission today, whether in music, literature, or any of the arts or the humanities, has to do with the preservation of difference without, at the same time, sinking into the desire to dominate. When you say, "There's a German identity, or there's a German tradition," one has to admit that and acknowledge that they're not all the same; of course, what goes into the precise making of that tradition, whether it's English or German or Arab, that's another question—but I think one has to be able to say courageously, "Yes, there is an Egyptian or German or French or Jewish identity of some sort," which in itself is not pure. It itself is made up of different elements. But it has a coherent sound and personality or profile to it, on the one hand. And on the other hand, there's the need to say, "Yes, there is this identity," especially if you're a German or an Arab or a Jew or an American, and then to say, "Yes, it's not only different, it's also better." I mean, it's the built-in logic of the bloody thing. Therefore, the humanistic mission has to be able to maintain difference but without the domination and bellicosity that normally accompany affirmations of identity. And that's very, very hard to do. We are going against every conceivable current that exists.

DB: Of course, but this is why the music is so important and, in some way, in the meaning of it, so inaccessible.

AG: But the most overriding parallel and paradox in your mutual histories is the complexity of your cultural backgrounds. Edward, you grew up as a Christian Arab in Palestine and Egypt. Daniel, you grew up as the grandson of Russian Jewish immigrants in Argentina and in Israel, and you both had, growing up, very clearly instilled in you, Beethoven—if we can use him as a model—as a kind of cultural ideal. And I think the commonality there is that you come from very complicated mixed cultural backgrounds, to which you've added yet one more layer, this bond for European intellectual tradition, and you embrace all of them.

EWS: Yes, but that's very hard to maintain. I don't really have very great confidence that it can be replicated. That's, in a sense, the tragedy of a Barenboim: he's trying to do something that has universal meaning but is rooted in something so particular that it cannot now be duplicated. The paradox of humans is that you're trying to talk about the human at the same time that the human is individual. Take, for example, a performance of the Beethoven Third Piano Concerto. The Third Piano Concerto is in the playing of it, in the performing of it, measure by measure, note by note, instant by instant, and what you're putting together is a unique whole, of which you might say, "Okay. Beethoven did that." Fine. But lying on a page, it has no existence. You have to come to the performance. How does one extend that? That is the problem. Beyond the ultra-individuality of the experience, how does one give it a kind of resonance beyond itself? How does one give it a kind of extension?

DB: I believe that there comes now, I suppose, the mystical element in music.

EWS: You see, I don't have that. Try it. Try and convince me.

DB: I believe that when all things are right on the stage—when the playing, the expression, everything becomes permanently, constantly interdependent—it becomes indivisible. And this is the mystical, because this is the same idea of religion, of God: that there's suddenly something that you cannot divide anymore. The experience of music-making is that, in a way. It's not religious in the sense that one prays to it, but it's comparable to religion in the sense that it cannot be divided. And when this actually happens, I believe that the active listener, who is sensitive, can communicate with that. This is what I mean by the mystical.

EWS: I agree with that. But I think what you have to include in it, Daniel, is the element of loss. There's a tragic element to it. You know, Shelley has a wonderful phrase, in which he says that the poetic mind, while it is in the act of creation, is like a fading coal. What you have to include, I think, in what you just said, is the fact that it's a kind of extraordinarily energetic and committed battle to keep something alive which is constantly flagging.

DB: Sound is exactly that. Sound, in many degrees, tends to go to silence.

EWS: Yes. So, necessary to the sound is, at the same time, its very opposite. But I need to connect it to the larger silence—to this very particular kind of organized experience, which you call mystical. I say, "No, you can actually analyze elements." Of course, the animating force of it is, in some way, kind of mysterious; I think we're going to have to admit that. But still, it is something that you can feel. You can define it, but you can't calculate the full synthesis.

DB: It's the difference between the whole and the sum of the parts.

EWS: Right, right. Absolutely.

DB: It's the same thing in mathematics.

EWS: But, Daniel, the synthesis is very precarious. That's all I'm saying. It reminds me of a story I want to tell you. There's an Indian actress and cookbook author, whom you may know quite well: Madhur Jaffrey. Now, the interesting thing about her name is that Madhur is a Hindu name, and Jaffrey is a Muslim name, and the combination of Hindu and Muslim is, as you know, extremely charged. So, she tells a story of once getting a phone call, and the man says, "Is this Madhur Jaffrey?" in a very strong Indian accent. She said, "Yes." And so he said, "So, how come?" I think that's the question. You said, "How much?" I say, "How come?"

AG: I want to go back quite early in our conversation because, as a listener, I reacted exactly as you did, Edward. You used exactly the right word, which is the animation of these performances and the degree to which they give urgency. And of course, this is where it veers into the mystical. The root of animation is "anima," and in that moment, it's alive. And I just wanted to ask why you resist the mysticism of that.

EWS: Well, you see the problem with mysticism and anything that suggests the divine or something extra-human, is that it, I think, brings it down a notch.

DB: It's metaphysical more than mystical; meta- goes beyond the physical, and it goes beyond the rational. Can you say meta-rational?

EWS: Yes, of course. I would prefer that—meta-rational. The animation of sound is opposed to what is inanimate and what is lifeless. There isn't a dead moment in these performances. And so, that becomes a goal in itself: to make it so alive that nothing in the score is left just supine or implicit—in the bad sense of the word, unstated. You get a sense of full statement, without necessarily having imposed on it all the nonsensical claptrap, which historically has been associated, especially and uniquely, with Beethoven. All you have to do is look at what Wagner said about Beethoven to find all these declarations of a high kind of destiny and humanism, and so on. And of course, a lot of it is given legitimization by the Ninth Symphony. But what I was talking about was something that was a kind of ultimate movement, where you have an image of constant energy: organized, articulated, with a point to it, without being able to specify what the point is. Certainly the music moves to a conclusion in every case; especially in Beethoven, there's this very tremendously fervent conclusion. And it's a very precious thing. And you can't associate it, for example, with reproduced sound; you can't associate it with records. You agree? When you think back to an important moment in your musical history or intellectual history, you don't think back to a record. You think back to an actual performance, a musical occasion.

DB: There are a few exceptions. I think some of the Furtwängler live-performance recordings have that quality, especially the ones just before or during the war.

EWS: No, but I mean, quite literally, Daniel, that they are memories, they're not the actual.

DB: Of course.

EWS: That's all I'm saying. So, they are something from which something has departed and that gives them their glow in a way.

DB: This is why sound has such a philosophical dimension for me, in a paradoxical way. The eternal value of Beethoven, of music in general, of sound, is because the works are of a certain duration, and when they are finished, the sound disappears and does not live in our world. Where does sound disappear? Where did the sounds of the Eighth Symphony that we played last night disappear? Physically, disappeared, they're finished. And yet, if we were to sit today and play again the Eighth Symphony, we could bring them back, at will. It wouldn't be the same; it wouldn't be the same sound; it would be the same river with different waters. And this is what gives music its particular sense of eternity. And this is why you can create with great stillness of expression; you can create the feeling of eternity with sound in a couple of seconds. Sometimes a held chord, you know, you feel could actually go on forever. It's the art of illusion. There's an element of creating illusion with music, with sound, which gives us this meta-rational quality.

AG: We talked about the ability of music to express ideals beyond itself, which is always an underlying issue in Beethoven. And I was struck yesterday by the fact that we were listening to this music being played by what is essentially an opera orchestra, which, first of all, comes to this music through knowledge of *Fidelio*—including the wonderful moment you articulated earlier—and so, its knowledge comes from knowledge of those sorts of highly dramatic junctures. We have spoken about this process of transformation and triumph in Beethoven. Hearing the Fourth and the Fifth Symphonies in the same night is very instructive, actually, because something of it happens on a very different scale in each piece. How much of this philosophical ideal of emerging from darkness to light is an actual element in performing Beethoven?

DB: Well, in Beethoven, that's very strong. The Germans have had a great preoccupation with old Greek mythology, as we all know. Wagner also was drawn to the idea of catharsis, which was essential to Beethoven. And it is not a coincidence that the funeral march in the *Eroica* is the second movement and not the last movement. In other words, that is seen also—death, in that respect, a tragic element—as a transitory element and not as a final. Only Tchaikovsky, who was much more immersed, if you will, in subjective thinking and feeling, could write the *Pathétique* Symphony and end it with the gloom that it does. With Beethoven, there is an active necessity to animate even the most negative thing—in this case, a funeral march—and to bring the symphony to a close with an affirmation of triumph or positive expression. And then, the Fourth Symphony is a perfect case. When it starts, it is basically a search for tonality. This is why the whole principle of harmony is so important in this piece. But you have to go through darkness in order to see the light. If you're always in light, you don't see it anymore. And this is the whole element of struggle—the courage to go through darkness in order to achieve light—which is the same in music as it is in every psychoanalytical process, as it is in every political process, in everything.

EWS: But you know, in particular, I thought something else in the relationship that Ara referred to between the Fourth and the Fifth Symphonies, which was quite striking; and that is that the musical world in the Fourth Symphony is completely different from the Fifth Symphony.

DB: It's another idiom.

EWS: It's incredible. I mean, I think that perhaps, in all the symphonies, the transition from the Fourth to the Fifth, perhaps because they were performed in the same evening, is the most dramatic of all.

DB: I also find the transition from the Sixth to the Seventh to be very dramatic.

EWS: Let's look at those: Four to Five, and then, Six to Seven. As a performer, obviously, you have to martial the forces differently to play it, to produce different sounds, to produce different moods. Something has happened between the end of the Fourth Symphony and the beginning of the Fifth? Obviously, it's a musical transformation of a very dramatic kind. But I just wonder whether that's sufficient to explain it. Would you, as a performer, adduce here a psychological event, some revelation, some need for Beethoven to make the leap from the Fourth to the Fifth? The Fourth is relatively sunny, but not exactly uncomplicated. I remember the animation that you brought to the last movement of the Fourth. This is a very active, busy, energetic motion. But from there to the beginning of the Fifth is really stunning. So, what occurs to me is two possibilities: that something has occurred, or that the need in Beethoven is so strong for a total contrast that he has to go to such an extreme to produce it in the Fifth. That may be the only explanation necessary—that he works by contrasts.

DB: I think so. Look at the Second Symphony, in many ways a very positive, sunny work.

EWS: And then the Third.

DB: But the Second was written at a time when he was in total despair, when he wrote the Heiligenstadt Testament, when he wanted to commit suicide.

EWS: What you're really pointing to is a need for opposites and contrasts, all the time. Is there any other analogy for it?

DB: I don't think so. It's unique to Beethoven. And I think it has to do with the historical development of music. Bach is, for me, an epic composer: everything builds up, one layer over the other. The fugue is the perfect example of that. And then comes the sonata form, which is basically dramatic and works on contrasts. It started with Haydn and Mozart and was, actually, developed by Beethoven to its utmost. There's nobody who developed the sonata form further than Beethoven.

EWS: But also what is implied in that is that, because the sonata form ends, there's a time when people don't write in sonata form anymore. So, to your ears as a performer and musician, what does the epoch of the sonata form signify? Is it just a passage of time, and then the ear gets tired of that particular form?

DB: Well, I think it has to do with the Zeitgeist. With Bach, it has to do with serving God and all this epic nature of the music; then the dramatic sonata form goes hand in hand with the French Revolution and all that. And then comes the symphonic poem and the music dramas of Wagner, which have to do with the subjectivity of the Romantic movement.

EWS: Yes, but that's it. Don't you think that, in a sense, the end of the sonata form is really the end of a period where certain aesthetic forms can be taken for granted by the audience. Wagner, in a sense, has to invent his own forms—I mean, the gigantic structures of his operas. And then later, of course, in the Strauss tone poems, these are the composer providing not just the music but also the literary and literal justification for it, which Beethoven doesn't seem to have required.

DB: Beethoven was an absolute musician.

AG: Yes, Beethoven was an absolute musician, but even in his own time, there's the famous E. T. A. Hoffmann review of the Fifth Symphony, published barely two years after the first performance in 1809, in which Hoffmann writes: "Beethoven's music induces terror, fright, horror, and pain and awakens that endless longing which is the essence of romanticism." He describes it in what we would now consider pure nineteenth-century terms. So, it was already understood in his time as being beyond absolute, to a degree.

EWS: Yes. And I think also Beethoven, unlike Mozart and Haydn, was certainly a more philosophical composer. If you look at the evidence that we have from his friends, from his library and the things he read, he took what he read much more seriously than, say, Mozart did.

DB: Mozart had an instinctive understanding of life. When you look at the Da Ponte operas, there's such a wisdom of life. It's not pure Da Ponte; it has to have been Mozart as well. But I think it was more intuitive.

EWS: Yes, more intuitive. Beethoven was always searching. He kept notebooks. He copied down quotations that meant a lot to him. He was obviously inspired by ideas in the French Revolution. He was inspired by ideas about rapturous states, and he seems to have been very interested in mystical experience, I mean, in a rational way because he was a man of rationality. He was an Enlightenment man, in a much more explicit way, I think, than Mozart.

DB: But from this point of view, the most important thing about Mozart is that he was the first pan-European, really. He spoke languages: he spoke French; he spoke Italian; he spoke German. He wrote music with all these languages, whereas Beethoven was much more limited to the German hemisphere.

AG: If you look at pieces like Mozart's *Magic Flute* and Haydn's *The Creation*, both are explicitly representations of the transformation from darkness to light.

EWS: Yes, but they take place within frameworks that are not theirs; in the sense, that, in the case of Mozart, it's the Masonic confection of so-called Egyptian mysteries that he was very close to, and then Haydn's source was the Christian Bible itself. That's what I'm trying to say. There's a greater reliance on what is conventional, accepted, in the society. With Beethoven, the feeling is that of trying to piece together a philosophy from fragments that exist around him. He was very influenced by Goethe; obviously, Schiller means a lot to him; and he was preparing his own music for that. But you have a sense that Beethoven is sustained by an abiding, rational faith. I think, obviously that's why people keep coming back to him: there's a faith in humanity, which slowly disappears over the course of the century into private myths—if you think of Wagner—or into music, as Adorno describes in the case of Schoenberg, that's totally immobilized. It doesn't have a social or humanistic message anymore. As I said earlier, I think that's the stark contrast between the trumpet in *Fidelio* and, say, the atonal world of Schoenberg, where music can really resist that kind of acceptance.

AG: Do you accept that premise, Daniel?

DB: Absolutely.

EWS: Daniel's work is so compelling that it provokes a lot of questions—how do you, as a performer, feel about the curatorial aspect of what you do? You are the custodian of a great musical past, the Western musical heritage—the symphonies of Beethoven, the operas of Mozart, etc., on one hand—but also an active participant in the music of your time. How do you find a balance between those two sorts of responsibilities?

DB: I'm very interested and fascinated by so much music of today—composers like Carter, Boulez, Birtwistle. This is very important. I wouldn't want to live without them. But for me, Beethoven's not a composer of the past. Beethoven is not a contemporary composer. He's a modern composer. He has, you know, the same importance as something that is being written today, sometimes even more so. And I think that the most important thing is to arrive at a way to play Beethoven with a sense of discovery, as if it were being written today, and to have enough understanding about the new pieces by Boulez and company, so that you play them with the kind of familiarity that one associates with the works of the past.

EWS: But what about the pathos of the past? To me, that's very important. In other words, what is the past as past. And I think that one respects it and admires it and cares about it because it is past, not only because one can bring it up to date and show its connections with the modern. Do you understand what I'm trying to say? I think there's a kind of ruthlessness in history, which I feel is deeply embedded in the human experience. One feels that certain things are irrecoverable because they are past. I'll give you an example. In the Berg Concerto, in the final movement, the appearance of the Bach chorale is profoundly moving, precisely because it's so at odds with the material that's presented there, not because he has used it in his concerto, but because of the glaring contrast between the two. Surely, you feel that as well, don't you, even with Beethoven?

DB: I'm actually bothered by this Bach chorale.

EWS: Oh, you are. Well, that's interesting.

DB: I'm bothered by it, because I find that somehow it introduces a foreign element into the structure, into the piece.

EWS: But what if you were told by him, as I think he would say, "Well, I intended it."

DB: Yes, I'm sure. Well, I'm still bothered by it.

EWS: The bother, itself, is what I'm interested in, I mean, that that could also be a part of the aesthetic experience: these jarring messages that come in and disrupt what could be a utopian, ideal situation.

DB: But, you know, this is like in architecture. You can argue the merit of beauty of angularity verses roundness. And there is beauty in both of them. And I think that the most wonderful thing about the aesthetic experience, of music in particular, is that you go from one to the other. You go from angularity to roundness, and you go from masculinity to femininity, and you go from heroic to lyric, all these things. And in a sense, to learn to live with that is to learn to live with the fluidity of life. In that respect, it is a parallel to real life. You must have the courage to accept the fluidity of elements that happen in development. Every development, every departure, means leaving something behind.

EWS: No, I disagree with that. I really think that there are certain things that one mustn't accept. And for me, for example, Beethoven is, to a certain extent, about that. That is to say, there is resistance. In other words, I don't think everything can be resolved.

DB: Of course not.

EWS: And I'm more interested in what can't be resolved and what is irreconcilable. I mean, that's what I think, in the contrast between aesthetics and politics, is that if every aesthetic phenomenon could be somehow recuperated to a political one, then in the end, there's no resistance; whereas I think it's useful, at times, to think of the aesthetic as an indictment of the political and that it's a stark contrast, forcefully made, to inhumanity, to injustice. And I think that's what people respond to in Beethoven. You do, too. So, in my opinion, it's dangerous to say, "Well, you know, that's part of life." There are parts of life that one doesn't want to accept.

DB: No, but it's part of life that you go from one to the other.

EWS: What gives your performances such power is precisely that they keep reminding one that this is A, and it's not B. It's precisely because it's so A that you can't say it's B. For me, as somebody who cares so deeply about music, a very important part of the practice of music is that music, in some profound way, is perhaps the final resistance to the acculturation and the commodification of everything.

New York,
December 14, 2000

Germans, Jews, and Music
by Daniel Barenboim

The cruelty of memory manifests itself in remembering
what is dispelled in forgetfulness.—NAGUIB MAHFOUZ

This statement by Naguib Mahfouz expresses something that I believe is very important for the relationship between Germans and Jews, since, with respect to each other, both are dealing with the problem of the past. Certain matters require the generosity of forgetfulness, and others demand the honesty of remembrance. From my point of view this is the difficulty with postwar German generations, although I have never had any personal experience of xenophobia or anti-Semitism in Germany. A recent statement by a well-known Berlin politician about "the Jew Barenboim" was made in a context that had nothing to do with Judaism, and I interpret it as a sign of his misunderstanding of Judaism.*

Editor's note: Klaus Landowsky, the leader of the Christian Democratic Union in the Berlin Senate, caused an outcry toward the end of 2000 when he talked about the difficulty of choosing the right person to run the Berliner Staatsoper, whose director was then, and still is, Daniel Barenboim. In the presence of a reporter, Mr. Landowsky said, "On the one hand, you have the young Karajan, Christian Thielemann. On the other, you have the Jew Barenboim."

It is true that Judaism is not easily explained: it is part religion, part tradition, part nation, and partly an immensely various people. It is hard to deal with, as much for the Jews themselves as for everyone else, and especially for a country like Germany, which has such a horrible common history with the Jews. Sadly, after spending years in Germany, I have a deeper and deeper impression that this part of German history has not been assimilated or understood by many Germans. Such ignorance could lead to a new anti-Semitism or to philo-Semitism, which would be as wrong as anti-Semitism. I don't believe in collective guilt, especially not after so many generations have passed, and therefore I have no problem living and working in Germany. But at the same time I expect every German not to forget this part of his country's history, and to be especially careful in considering it. Each German will be able to do this, however, only if he has an understanding of his own self and the past that helped to form it; for if you suppress an important element of yourself, you are constrained in your dealings with others. Such thoughts lead to the question of German identity and to the general question of what an identity consists of. Is there really only one identity for a person or for a people? The Jewish tradition has two distinct tendencies: the more fundamental one, represented by the philosophers and poets and scholars who were interested only in Jewish issues and in the Jewish *Weltanschauung*; and the other tendency associated with great figures such as Spinoza or Einstein, and to a certain extent also Heinrich Heine, and which applied the traditions of Jewish thinking to other cultures, including German culture, and to other issues. It is not difficult to see how a double identity developed among Jews.

In my opinion it is impossible for anyone at the beginning of the twenty-first century to believably claim a single identity.

One difficulty of our times is that people restrict their concerns to ever smaller details, and that they often have little sense of how things are intermingled with one another, and together form part of a whole. The Germans have given the world so much by way of spiritual enlightenment—we have only to think of Bach, Beethoven, Wagner, Heine, Goethe, to name just a few—but perhaps the horrific experiences of the Nazi era, and shortly after, have made it particularly difficult for a German in the year 2001 to confront his own history as a whole.

I look at the question of identity both as a musician and from the perspective of my own history. I was born in Argentina, my grandparents were Russian Jews, I grew up in Israel, and I have lived most of my adult life in Europe. I think in the language that I happen to speak at a particular moment. I feel German when I conduct Beethoven, and Italian when I conduct Verdi. This does not give me a feeling of being untrue to myself; quite the contrary. The experience of playing very different styles of music can be remarkably illuminating. When you have learned and played a Debussy pianissimo, and when you then return to a Beethoven pianissimo, you know even better what the differences are, and you realize you are dealing with two entirely different sounds. With Debussy the pianissimo has to be bodiless, and with Beethoven it has to have a physical core of expression and sound.

It is only natural to find excursions into different cultures valuable, but of course German culture is something extraordinary, and there should be no false modesty about it. If you understand Beethoven as somebody who was at the same time German and universal, it also becomes apparent that Germans, much more than those of many other nations, have occupied themselves with past cultures, for example with Greek mythology, literature, and philosophy. All of Beethoven's work is based to some degree on the Greek principle of catharsis, which reflects a typical German attitude: one should not fear to enter the dark and reemerge into the light. The first movement of the Fourth Symphony, for example, starts from the depths of chaos and finds an extraordinary way to order and jubilation.

I found the speech of the president of Germany, Johannes Rau, on November 9 last year especially apt when he spoke about the differences between nationalism and patriotism. He said: "Patriotism can flourish only where racism and nationalism are given no quarter. We should never mistake patriotism for nationalism. A patriot is one who loves his homeland. A nationalist is one who scorns the homelands of others."

These seem to me very important points. I believe that many Germans lost their sense of patriotism, their affection for their country, during the second half of the twentieth century and did so partly out of fear of nationalism. This is unfortunate. The change took place during a time of large-scale immigration, when more foreigners wanted to come, or felt compelled to come, to Germany than ever before. Germany opened its gates and made use of the immigrants without having acquired the tolerance of a state based on immigration, such as, for example, Argentina or the United States. The attitudes of many Germans who are hostile to foreigners seem to me to derive from the fact that the last two or three generations of Germans have not adequately learned what immigration means. They fail to understand that it is possible to have more than one identity at the same time and to accept that people of foreign origin, with foreign customs and a foreign culture, can become part of one's own land without their threatening one's identity as a German.

The best example of this specific German problem is the current situation in Berlin, in which some people fear that their capital is becoming multicultural, or multidimensional. This fear surely stems from a past that has not been entirely assimilated. Berlin was the only divided city in Germany, and the two parts of the city had unusual external support; both the Federal Republic of Germany and the German Democratic Republic considered Berlin a city with a special status. My hope is that Berlin will not lose its special status because of reunification—on the contrary. Because of the forty-year-long division and the existence of the East and the West side by side, Berlin, in my view, has a unique potential for encompassing differences, a potential that should now be made use of. Instead of complaining about the division caused by history, one should treat it as a positive force, for Berlin and also for the city's relations with the rest of Germany and with other countries. After all, Berlin is the only city where a delegation from Moscow will not feel wholly foreign in the West and, at the same time, a delegation from Washington will not feel wholly foreign in the East.

If we are to understand the phenomena of nature, or the qualities of human beings, or the relationship to a God or to some different, spiritual experience, we can learn much through music. Music is so very important and interesting to me because it is at the same time everything and nothing. If you wish to learn how to live in a democratic society, then you would do well to play in an orchestra. For when you do so, you know when to lead and when to follow. You leave space for others and at the same time you have no inhibitions about claiming a place for yourself. And despite this, or maybe precisely because of it, music is the best means of escape from the problems of human existence.

Germans, Jews, and Music

For me there is only one clear definition of music, by Ferruccio Busoni, who said: "Music is sonorous air." Everything else that is said about music refers to the different reactions that music evokes in people: it is felt to be poetic, or sensual, or spiritual, or emotional, or formally fascinating; the possibilities are countless. Since music is everything and nothing at the same time, it therefore can be easily abused, as it was by the Nazis. At the West-Eastern Divan Workshop in Weimar, musicians from Israel and the Arab countries have in recent years worked together and shown that rapprochements and friendships hitherto thought impossible may be achieved through music; but this does not mean that music will solve the problems of the Middle East. Music can be the best school for life, and at the same time the most effective way to escape from it.

The New York Review of Books
March 29, 2001

Barenboim and the Wagner Taboo
by Edward W. Said

The public performance of Richard Wagner's music has always been banned informally in Israel, although his music is
sometimes played on the radio and recordings are available in
Israeli shops. To many Israeli Jews, Wagner's music—rich, extraordinarily complex, extraordinarily influential in the musical world—has come to symbolize the horrors of German
anti-Semitism. Nevertheless, he was an unquestionably great
genius when it came to the theater and to music. He revolu-
tionized our whole conception of opera; he totally transformed
the tonal musical system; and he contributed ten great masterpieces, ten operas that remain among the very great sum-
mits of Western music. The challenge he presents, not just to
Israeli Jews but to everyone, is how to admire and perform his
music on the one hand and, on the other hand, to separate
from that his odious writings and the use made of them by the
Nazis. As Daniel Barenboim has frequently pointed out, none
of Wagner's operas have any immediately anti-Semitic material in them; more bluntly, the Jews he hated and wrote about
in his pamphlets are simply not at all to be found *as Jews* or
Jewish characters in his musical works. Many critics have im-

puted an anti-Semitic presence in some characters that Wagner treats with contempt and derision in his operas: but such
accusations can only be imputations of anti-Semitism, not instances of it, although the resemblance between caricatures
of Jews that were common at the time and Beckmesser, a
derisory character in Wagner's only comic opera *Die Meistersinger von Nürnberg* are actually quite close. Still, Beckmesser
himself is a German Christian character in the opera, most
certainly not Jewish. Clearly, Wagner made the distinction in
his own mind between Jews in reality and Jews in his music,
since he was voluble about the former in his writing, and silent
on them in the latter.

Wagner's works have, therefore, by common consent been
left unperformed in Israel, until July 7, 2001. Daniel Barenboim, who was leading the Berlin State Opera on tour in Israel
for the three consecutive concerts to be presented in Jerusalem, had originally scheduled a performance of Act 1 of Wagner's opera *Die Walküre* for the July 7 concert, but had been
asked to change it by the director of the Israel Festival. Barenboim substituted a program of Schumann and Stravinsky, and
then, after playing those, turned to the audience and proposed
a short extract from Wagner's *Tristan und Isolde* as an encore.
He opened the floor to a discussion, which ensued with people
for and against. In the end, Barenboim said he would play the
piece but suggested that those who were offended could leave,
which some in fact did. By and large though, the Wagner was
well received by a rapturous audience of about twenty-eight
hundred Israelis and, I am sure, extremely well performed.

A furor, however, erupted and the attacks on Barenboim
have continued for several months. On July 25 it was reported
that the Knesset committee on culture and education "urged
Israel's cultural bodies to boycott the conductor . . . for performing music by Hitler's favorite composer at Israel's premier

cultural event until he apologises." The attacks on Barenboim by the minister of culture and other luminaries have been venomous, even though despite his birth and early childhood in Argentina, he himself has always thought of himself as an Israeli. He grew up there, he went to Hebrew schools, he carries an Israeli passport along with his Argentinian one. Besides, he has always been thought of as a major cultural asset to Israel, having been a central figure in the country's musical life for years and years, despite the fact that since his teens he has lived mostly in Europe and the United States. This has been largely a result of his work, which has continuously taken him around the world to conduct and play the piano in Berlin, Paris, London, Vienna, Salzburg, Bayreuth, New York, Chicago, Buenos Aires, among many other cities.

Barenboim is a complex figure, which also explains the furor over what he did. All societies are made up of a majority of average citizens who follow all the established patterns and a tiny number who by virtue of their talent and their independent inclinations are not at all average, and in many ways are a challenge and even an affront to the usually docile majority. The problems occur when the perspective of the docile majority tries to reduce, simplify, and codify the complex and unroutine people who are a tiny minority. This clash inevitably occurs—large numbers of people cannot easily tolerate someone who is noticeably different, more talented, more original, than they are—and inevitably causes rage and irrationality in the majority. Look what Athens did to Socrates, because he was a genius who taught young people how to think independently and skeptically: he was sentenced to death. The Amsterdam Jews excommunicated Spinoza because his ideas were too much for them. Galileo was punished by the church. Al-Hallaj was crucified for his insights. And so it has gone for centuries. Barenboim is a gifted, extremely unusual figure who crossed too many lines and violated too many of the many taboos that bind Israeli society.

Barenboim has every conceivable gift available to someone who wants to be a great soloist and conductor—a perfect memory, competence and even brilliance in technical matters, a winning manner before the public, and above all, an enormous love of what he does. Nothing musical is beyond him or too difficult for him to master. Living an itinerant life and achieving the kind of recognition he has had has come not with a studious compliance with standards set by ordinary people but by exactly the opposite, that is, a regular flouting of conventions and barriers. Few important achievements in matters of art or science are accomplished by living within the boundaries designed to regulate social and political life.

Because he has lived abroad and traveled so much, and because he has a gift for languages (he can speak seven fluently), Barenboim is in a sense at home everywhere and nowhere. His visits to Israel are limited to a few days a year, though he keeps in touch by phone and by reading the press. Another reason for his being at home everywhere and nowhere is that he seems capable of being at ease in many contrasting cosmopolitan locales, not just in the United States and Britain, but in Germany, where he spends most of his time now. One can imagine that for many Jews for whom Germany still represents what is most evil and anti-Semitic, Barenboim's residence there is a difficult pill to swallow, more particularly in that his chosen area of music to perform is the classical Austro-Germanic repertory, in which Wagner's operas are at the very center. Aesthetically of course, this is a sound, not to say absolutely predictable area for a classical musician to concentrate on: it includes the great works of Mozart, Haydn, Beethoven, Brahms, Schumann, Bruckner, Mahler, Wagner, Richard Strauss, plus, of course, many other composers in the French,

Russian, and Spanish repertory at which Barenboim has excelled. But the core is Austrian and German music, music that for some Jewish philosophers and artists has sometimes presented a great problem, especially since World War II. The great pianist Arthur Rubinstein, a friend and mentor of Barenboim's, more or less refused ever to go to Germany and play there because, he would say, as a Jew it was hard for him to be in a country that had slaughtered so many of his people. So already there developed a sense of estrangement in many of Barenboim's Israeli admirers about his residence in Berlin, in the heart of the former capital of the Third Reich, which many living Jews still consider to bear within it today the marks of its former evil.

All of the great composers in one way or another were political, and held quite strong political ideas; some of them, in the case of the early Beethoven who adulated Napoleon as a great conqueror, or Debussy who was a right-wing French nationalist, were quite reprehensible from today's perspective. Haydn, as another example suggests, was a servile employee of his aristocratic patron Prince Esterhazy, and even the greatest of all geniuses, Johann Sebastian Bach, was often fawning at the table or at the court of an archbishop or a duke.

We don't much care about these things today because they belong to a relatively remote and distant period. None of them offends us quite so sharply as one of Thomas Carlyle's racist pamphlets about blacks in the 1860s, but there are two other factors that need consideration as well. One is that music as an art form is not like language: notes don't mean something stable, the way a word like "cat" or "horse" does. Second, music for the most part is transnational; it goes beyond the boundaries of a nation or a nationality and language. You don't have to know German to appreciate Mozart, and you don't have to be French to read a score by Berlioz. You have to know music, which is a very specialized technique acquired with painstaking care quite apart from subjects like history or literature, although I would argue that the context and traditions of individual works of music have to be understood for purposes of true comprehension and interpretation. In some ways, music is like algebra, but not quite, as the case of Wagner testifies.

Were he a minor composer or someone who composed his work hermetically or at least quietly, Wagner's contradictions would have been slightly easier to accept and tolerate. But he was incredibly voluble, filling Europe with his pronouncements, projects, and music, all of which went together and all of which were larger than life, more impressive, more designed to overwhelm and compel the listener than those of every other composer. At the center of all his work was his own fantastically self-concerned, even narcissistic self, which he considered in no uncertain way to embody the essence of the German soul, its destiny, and its privileges. Wagner sought controversy, demanded attention, did everything for the cause of Germany and himself, which he conceived of in the most extreme revolutionary terms. His was to be a new music, a new art, a new aesthetic, and it was to embody the tradition of Beethoven and Goethe, and, typically, it was to transcend them in a new, universal synthesis. No one in the history of art has attracted more attention, no one more writing, no one more commentary. Wagner was ready-made for the Nazis (he died in 1883), but he was also welcomed as a hero and a great genius by other musicians who understood that his contributions utterly changed the course of Western music. During his lifetime he had a special opera house, almost a shrine, built for him and the performance of only his operas in the small town of Bayreuth. Bayreuth and the Wagner family were dear to Hitler's heart, and to add a further complexity to the matter,

Barenboim and the Wagner Taboo

Richard Wagner's grandson Wolfgang still controls the summer festival at which Barenboim has conducted regularly for almost two decades.

Barenboim is in no way a fully fledged political figure but he made his unhappiness with Israel's occupation clear, and so in early 1999 he became the first Israeli to offer his services gratis to play a concert at Bir Zeit University on the West Bank. I agree with him that ignorance is not an adequate political strategy for a people, and therefore, each in his own way must understand and know the forbidden "other"; that reason, understanding, and intellectual analysis, and not the organization and encouragement of collective passions such as those that seem to impel fundamentalists, are the way to be a citizen.

The irrational condemnation and the blanket denunciation of complex phenomena such as Wagner is indiscriminate and finally unacceptable, just as for Arabs, it has been a foolish and wasteful policy for so many years to use phrases like "the Zionist entity" and completely refuse to understand and analyze Israel and Israelis on the grounds that their existence must be denied because they caused the Palestinian *nakba*. History is a dynamic thing, and if we expect Israeli Jews not to use the Holocaust to justify appalling human rights abuses of the Palestinian people, we too have to go beyond such idiocies as saying that the Holocaust never took place, and that Israelis are all, man, woman, and child, doomed to our eternal enmity and hostility. Politicians can talk all their usual nonsense and do what they want, and so can professional demagogues. But for intellectuals, artists, and free citizens, there must always be room for dissent, for alternative views, for ways and possibilities to challenge the tyranny of the majority and, at the same time and most importantly, to advance human enlightenment and liberty.

This idea is not easily dismissed as a "Western" import and

therefore inapplicable to Arab and Muslim, or for that matter, Jewish societies and traditions. It is a universal value to be found in every tradition that I know of. Every society has conflicts in it between justice and injustice, ignorance and knowledge, freedom and oppression. The point is not simply to belong to one side or the other because one is told to, but to choose carefully and to make judgments that render what is just and due to every aspect of the situation. The purpose of education is not to accumulate facts or memorize the "correct" answer, but rather to learn how to think critically *for oneself*.

In the Israeli case about Wagner and Barenboim, how many writers, musicians, poets, painters would remain before the public if their art was judged by their moral behavior? And who is to decide what level of ugliness and turpitude can be tolerated in the artistic production of any given artist? For a mature mind it should be possible to hold together in one's mind two contradictory facts: that Wagner was a great artist, and second, that Wagner was a disgusting human being. Unfortunately, one cannot have one fact without the other. This is not to say that artists shouldn't be morally judged for their immorality or evil practices; it is to say that an artist's work cannot be judged solely on those grounds and banned accordingly.

During the heated Knesset debate a year ago as to whether Israeli high school students should or should not have the option to read Mahmoud Darwish, many of us took the vehemence with which the idea was attacked as a sign of how closed-minded orthodox Zionism was. In deploring the opponents of the idea that young Israelis would benefit from reading a major Palestinian author, many people argued that history and reality couldn't be hidden forever, and that censorship of that kind had no place in the educational curriculum. Wagner's music presents a similar problem, although there can be no denying the fact that the terrible associations with his music and ideas are a genuine trauma for those who feel that the composer was, in a sense, ready-made for appropriation by the Nazis. Yet at some point with a major composer like Wagner, blocking out his existence will not work. If it hadn't been Barenboim who performed his music in Israel on July 7, 2001, it would have been someone else a little later. A complex reality always bursts in on attempts to seal it out. The question then becomes how to understand the Wagner phenomenon, rather than whether or not to recognize its existence, which is an inadequate and obviously insufficient response.

In the Arab context, the campaign against "normalization" with Israel, while more urgent and actual a challenge—after all, Israel is practicing modes of daily collective punishment and murder against an entire people, whose land it has illegally occupied for thirty-four years—has some similar features with the Israeli taboos against Palestinian poetry and Wagner. Our problem is that Arab governments have economic and political relationships with Israel while groups of individuals have tried to impose a blanket ban on all contacts with Israelis. The ban on normalization lacks coherence since its *raison d'être,* Israel's oppression of the Palestinian people, hasn't been alleviated by the campaign: how many Palestinian homes have been protected from demolition by anti-normalization measures, and how many Palestinian universities have been able to give their students instruction because anti-normalization has been in place? None at all, alas, which is why I have said that it is better for a distinguished Egyptian intellectual to come to Palestine in solidarity with his/her Palestinian comrades, perhaps to teach or give a lecture or help at a clinic, than it is to sit at home preventing others from doing so. Complete anti-normalization is not an effective weapon for the powerless: its symbolic value is low, and its actual effect is merely passive and negative. Successful weapons of the weak—as in India, the American South, Vietnam, Malaysia, and elsewhere —have always been active, and even aggressive. The point is to make the powerful oppressor uncomfortable and vulnerable both morally as well as politically. Suicide bombing doesn't achieve this effect, and neither does anti-normalization, which in the case of the South African liberation struggle was used as a boycott against visiting academics in conjunction with a whole variety of other means.

That is why I believe we must try to penetrate the Israeli consciousness with everything at our disposal. Speaking or writing to Israeli audiences breaks *their* taboo against *us*. This fear of being addressed by what their collective memory has suppressed was what stirred up the whole debate about read-ing Palestinian literature. Zionism has tried to exclude non-Jews and we, by our unselective boycott of even the name "Israel," have actually *helped* rather than hindered this plan. And in a different context, it is why Barenboim's performance of Wagner, although genuinely painful for many who still suf-fer the real traumas of anti-Semitic genocide, has the salutary effect of allowing mourning to move on to another stage, i.e., toward the living of life itself, which must go on and cannot be frozen in the past. Perhaps I haven't caught all the many nu-ances of this complex set of issues, but the main point has to be that real life cannot be ruled by taboos and prohibitions against critical understanding and emancipatory experience. Those must always be given the highest priority. Ignorance and avoidance cannot be adequate guides for the present.

Al-Hayat,
August 15, 2001

Afterword

by Ara Guzelimian

These conversations exist in counterpoint with the enormous body of work from both Daniel Barenboim and Edward Said. Daniel Barenboim's recorded cycle of the complete Beethoven symphonies with the Berlin Staatskapelle (Teldec CDs) is almost exactly contemporary with the chapter on Beethoven. His two much-admired cycles of the complete Beethoven piano sonatas (the first on EMI, the more recent on Deutsche Grammophon) as well as his cycle of the Beethoven piano concertos (one with Otto Klemperer and the Philharmonia Orchestra, a later one with the Berlin Philharmonic, both sets on EMI) are also highly recommended. The recorded set of Beethoven's *Fidelio* (Teldec CD) includes an accompanying essay by Edward Said. Barenboim has also recorded practically the complete operas of Richard Wagner on compact disc (all on Teldec), with many of the Barenboim-led major stage productions in Bayreuth and Berlin now documented on video and DVD as well. Among his many other recordings, recent works by Pierre Boulez, Elliott Carter, and Luciano Berio are especially recommended (all with the Chicago Symphony Orchestra on Teldec).

Edward Said's *Musical Elaborations* (New York: Columbia

Afterword

University Press, 1991) collects a series of lectures at the University of California, Irvine, that encompass such subjects as the music criticism of Theodor Adorno, the presence of powerful musical imagery in Marcel Proust, and a variety of musical figures ranging from Glenn Gould to Richard Strauss. In addition, three recent anthologies are all invaluable for their essays and conversations on music and culture: *Power, Politics, and Culture* (New York: Pantheon Books, 2001); *Reflections on Exile and Other Essays* (Cambridge: Harvard University Press, 2000); and *The Edward Said Reader* (New York: Vintage Books, 2000). In addition, there is a fascinating chapter on Verdi's *Aida* in Said's *Culture and Imperialism* (New York: Alfred A. Knopf, 1993).

A NOTE ON THE AUTHORS

Edward W. Said was University Professor of English and
Comparative Literature at Columbia University and the author
of twenty-one books, including *Orientalism, Culture and
Imperialism*; and *The End of the Peace Process*.
His books have been published in thirty-six languages.
Edward Said died in 2003.

Daniel Barenboim was born in Buenos Aires and grew up in
Israel. He has been Music Director of the Chicago Symphony
Orchestra since 1991 and of the Deutsche Staatsoper in Berlin
since 1992. Barenboim began conducting with the New
Philharmonic Orchestra in London in 1967 and was musical
director of the Orchestre de Paris. He lives in Germany.

A NOTE ON THE EDITOR

Ara Guzelimian is Senior Director and Artistic Advisor at Carnegie Hall. He was previously Artistic Administrator of the Los Angeles Philharmonic and Aspen Music Festival and School. Active as a critic, writer, and radio producer, he is the host of the celebrated Carnegie Hall Talks, a series of conversations with great musicians.